Unquestioned Ease

Unquestioned Ease

Confronting Automaticity in Everyday Communication

Xiaowei Shi
Steve Mortenson

LEXINGTON BOOKS
Lanham • Boulder • New York • London

Published by Lexington Books
An imprint of The Rowman & Littlefield Publishing Group, Inc.
4501 Forbes Boulevard, Suite 200, Lanham, Maryland 20706
www.rowman.com

86-90 Paul Street, London EC2A 4NE, United Kingdom

Copyright © 2022 by The Rowman & Littlefield Publishing Group, Inc.

All rights reserved. No part of this book may be reproduced in any form or by any electronic or mechanical means, including information storage and retrieval systems, without written permission from the publisher, except by a reviewer who may quote passages in a review.

British Library Cataloguing in Publication Information Available

Library of Congress Cataloging-in-Publication Data Available

ISBN 9781793637963 (cloth: alk. paper) | ISBN 9781793637987 (paperback) | ISBN 9781793637970 (electronic)

∞™ The paper used in this publication meets the minimum requirements of American National Standard for Information Sciences—Permanence of Paper for Printed Library Materials, ANSI/NISO Z39.48-1992.

Contents

Preface   vii

1   Turning to a New Direction: Appreciating the Ease in Communication   1

2   When Communication Does Not Occur in a Smooth Progression   11

3   Identifying and Meeting the Emotional Challenges of Supportive Confrontation   29

4   What Happens When We Are Mindful in Communication?   47

5   Empirical Research on Mindful Communication   55

6   When You Can Never See the World in the Way I Do   77

7   Defusing Defenses and Speaking Skillfully   97

Bibliography   129

Author Index   143

Subject Index   147

About the Authors   151

Preface

In many ways, communicating with other people, especially when we are at cross-purposes with them, has never been more difficult. With so much toxic communication around issues such as race, gender, and political differences, it is more important than ever to develop tools and strategies for effective communication. We hope that by reading this book, you will have not only gained a new appreciation of communication with ease, we hope you have also gained some new ways to engage challenging subjects and people.

At first glance, the concept "communication with ease" may simply appear to be a coalescence of being easy, relaxed, or natural in conversations. After having examined it closely, however, now we see more details: that it takes courage to become aware of and manage our personal shadows and hidden preferences when talking with others, that it takes time to gain perspectives from each other, that it takes some strategic closure expressions when we want to exit a conversation, and that it embraces the possibilities of being changed while attempting to change the other.

This book is built on the extraordinary communication literature of implicit biases, mindfulness, and meaning construction during the past five decades. If, by any chance, you find the chapters in this book interesting and helpful for your own communication research, we would feel wholeheartedly grateful for that.

The main concepts in the AIM framework were developed in Dr. Shi's doctoral dissertation at Purdue University. Dr. Shi wishes to thank her advisor, Dr. Steve R. Wilson, for his important guidance in developing this line of thinking and his enduring mentorship throughout her academic career. Dr. Shi also wants to thank her husband, Feng Gao, for his unconditional love and support. Without his taking care of the family after school and during the weekend, which gives her time to write her chapters, this book would not be possible.

Dr. Mortenson would like to thank his colleagues at Blue Hen Leadership Program, Susan Luchey, Matt Creasy, and Julie Millisky, for all their help in the research and development of Strengths and Shadows and Supportive Confrontation. He also gives heartfelt thanks to all the University of Delaware students who have shared their stories, heartbreak, and triumphs in class

Your vulnerability, candor, and courage is the foundation of this work. Finally, Dr. Mortenson wishes to thank his wife Betsy and his children Chloe, Louis, and Joshua: you have been my greatest teachers and have helped me see more deeply into myself.

Finally, we both wish to thank our anonymous peer-review reviewers and our acquisitions editors (Ms. Nicolette Amstutz and Ms. Jessie Tepper) for giving us insightful feedback on the early versions of this manuscript. We also thank Dr. Sharon Felton for her careful proofreading of our manuscript. Thank you all!

Chapter 1

Turning to a New Direction

Appreciating the Ease in Communication

Xiaowei Shi and Steve Mortenson

Calling someone out, debating another's opinions, and making hard decisions with others—these are difficult steps to take in the best of times. Adding further to such challenges are several realities we often face in our daily interactions: our culture of intense political polarization, global health crises, and historic economic downturns. In short, we are faced with a lot of bad news and we will need to make many difficult decisions to navigate these challenges personally, professionally, and even nationally.

This book is about communication in conflict and confrontational interactions. It engages us to recognize when our intuitive thinking and emotional defenses are likely to interfere with clear and fair communication; it lays a framework to illustrate that it is possible to manage conflicts through exchanging views rather than demanding compliance; and it calls us to appreciate the ease in interpersonal communication at a *deeper* level.

To start our exploration, let's begin with a real-life conflict scenario between a student and a college professor (based on Dr. Shi's own experience). When reading it, can you imagine what would you say and do if you were Dr. Shi?

> In my teaching career, one event stays in my mind for a long time. It was a sunny afternoon at the end of a Communication Theory class. After all the other students had left, Cara[1] came to me and asked if she could do a makeup work for an assignment that was due two weeks ago.
>
> If I were to replay the scene now, I would ask her what happened and encourage her to talk more. This would give me time to understand her situation better. But that advice comes from hindsight. During the actual scenario, as a first-year Assistant Professor, I felt a need to immediately address her question. I reminded her of the syllabus policies, told her that she missed the deadline, and asked her why she often came in late or sometimes skipped a class.

As you can imagine, Cara got more and more frustrated. She asked me if she could receive some partial grade by doing a makeup. "No. Unless you had provided a legitimate excuse prior to the due date." Before I could finish my response, she shouted a curse word in my face and stormed out of the classroom.

I was genuinely shocked, standing there wordless. Later, the University's Office of Judicial Affairs met with Cara and discussed the inappropriate behavior she displayed.

Long story short, Cara came to apologize later in my office. Before our meeting, I mentally rehearsed what I would say to Cara. I wanted to be sincere and caring, and I also wanted to be firm and clear on what she needs to do for this course. Emotionally, I still felt uncomfortable to talk with her due to our prior encounter.

When we met, I did what I planned. I accepted her apology. Then I swiftly refocused our conversation to her study in this course. We discussed how she could catch up and improve her grades. During this time, I suppressed my feelings of unease; I simply tried to do what I was supposed to do—be a teacher who wanted her student to study well. Somehow, we started to click with each other, and we began to feel more comfortable. Cara revealed that her father would yell curse words to her when he got angry.

"I'm sorry; I shouldn't do that to you" Cara continued.

After Cara told me about her father, all the guarded feelings in me suddenly melted away. I felt as if there was no "wall" between us. I smiled to her, relaxed, and continued to talk with Cara.

This incident was not, by any reckoning, an easy or pleasant interpersonal interaction. For me, receiving an explicit profanity in my own classroom was totally unexpected and face-threatening. My social image as a college professor was challenged in a disrespectful manner. However, her behavior issues were already addressed in the university office. So, there was no need to focus on her impoliteness anymore. My primary goal in communication with Cara was to "show her the way," meaning that I want to show her the proper ways to handle a conflict.

For Cara, the automatic emotional outburst was her natural way to deal with a conflict. The automaticity of such a behavior involves an associative memory of a trigger and a typical action (e.g., cussing). Cara learned it from her father ("yelling curse words at her when he got angry").

As a reader, are you intrigued by this communication episode? What happened during this interaction that transformed an initial "crisis" mode of conflict in a later "comfortable" mode of conversing and connecting with each other? There must be some elements in the dialogue between Dr. Shi and Cara that worked subliminally to make them feel more at ease in the end. What are those elements? These explorative questions became the root of this book project.

A LOOK AT COMMUNICATION WITH EASE

In many situations like this case, we face the uncertainties of how to talk with another person. We are completely unaware of the other person's state of mind or of his or her past experiences. It becomes especially challenging when we must deal with conflicts coming from our friends, coworkers, or our loved ones because we find ourselves in a relationship web from which we cannot simply walk away. Besides conflict situations, there are other difficult communication tasks in everyday interactions, such as conveying bad news, giving unsolicited advice, and correcting other people's mistakes in a sensitive manner—no easy feat.

With these challenges in mind, let's start by taking a first look at the unique qualities of "ease" in communication. Our book title uses the term *ease* in two related senses. In this book, we convey an idea of questioning the ease in communication. *Ease* does not equate with automatic responses or thinking out loud. Rather, being at ease in communication refers to a desirable state, in which we talk with others in a comfortable and coordinated way that creates a smooth exchange of ideas on the issues at hand. As the following chapters will illustrate, ease in communication involves both issue-relevant thinking (or mindfulness) and coordinated acts. In other words, we, as communicators, collectively cultivate a sense of ease in communicating with others during the process of interacting with one another.

Second, this book challenges readers to investigate and to confront their own cognitive ease by looking into those hidden preferences, emotional defenses, and underlying beliefs about gender, relationships, and themselves with a new eye. As communicators, we first need to recognize that sometimes our intuitive senses are likely to lead us to make erroneous judgments. This book seeks to illustrate that our message choices in everyday conversation with friends, coworkers, and loved ones may further fuel systematic biases against others based on gender, age, or sociocultural backgrounds. The question is, "How can we recognize biased messages, and, in turn, make better message choices?"

COMMUNICATION AS INTERVENTION

Before turning to theory, we invite you to evaluate the following examples in terms of how we can use communication to intervene with hidden preferences in message choice.

As you can tell from these illustrative examples, skillfully confronting others about difficult topics is much more than simply saying "the right words." When facing a situation where the problem seems familiar and solutions appear obvious, we would probably have the mindset of "Why bother to think on our own" or "Let's get started!" At the moment, it almost becomes a rather stern challenge for us to pause the momentum, expressing a need to think or coordinate actions, such as "Let's not be misled by her age or gender" or "Before we start, can we decide how we are going to take turns to talk? Otherwise, we may" (see examples in table 1.1). In a word, skillfully confronting others requires both cognitive clarity and emotional calm.

This process involves recognizing those routine scripts, hidden biases, and resisting our own intuitive responses to a situation. As the first example has shown, what is "ready-to-use" in our mind may not be the best solution for a problem. When we are able to put ourselves in the right cognitive and emotional "frame," we can most skillfully employ the effective message strategies for advising, comforting, confronting, and influencing others.

Table 1.1. Illustrative Examples of Intervention Messages

Message with Hidden Preferences	Intervention
Message Based on Heuristics	
"For this kind of problem, there are a lot of ready-to-use solutions. Why bother to think on our own?"	"We are in a new situation. Let's find our own answer to this problem even though there are a lot of ready-to-use solutions."
Message Based on Hidden-Preference	
"She is so young. Can she lead such a big team?"	"Let's not be misled by her gender and young age for this position. The stereotypical view of 'leaders are men' can easily bias our judgment in hiring."
Message Based on Feelings	
"I can't bear with you. You are so rude. I'm very mad at you."	"I think you just made a good point even though you were raising your voice a lot. Let's calm down. Can you explain what you just said a little more?"
Messages Favoring Action Over Coordination	
"Let's do it." "Let's get started."	"Let's decide in advance how we are going to take turns to talk. Otherwise, we may get overwhelmed by our own way of thinking, get too emotional, or get stuck on one issue, and forget to consider all the steps we need to go through."

COGNITIVE EASE AND DUAL PROCESSING

The phenomenon that our mind has the capacity to do heuristics-based and reason-based dual processing has long been explored by researchers from multiple disciplines, including persuasion (Petty & Cacioppo, 1986), emotion interpretation (Barrett et al., 2019), judgment and decision-making (Tversky & Kahneman, 1974; Kahneman, 2011), and interpersonal influence (Dillard et al., 1989; Shi, 2013). What this line of research suggests is that, as communicators, we are not completely rational nor fully intuitive in responding to other's provocative arguments.

With regard to dual-processing capacity in our mind, on the one hand, we can rely on prior knowledge, heuristics, stereotypes, scripts, and schemas to deal with life and events. This process is rather quick and effortless. On the other hand, we also can expend effort to analyze the situation, people, and action before knowing how to respond. This second route of processing requires a certain level of systematic thinking to identify and integrate relevant information in order to make a well-adapted response. In his book *Thinking, Fast and Slow*, cognitive psychologist Kahneman (2011) described these two routes of thinking as System 1 ("fast thinking") and System 2 ("slow thinking").

According to Kahneman (2011), cognitive ease represents a continuum of attention and effort that we want to mobilize when assessing a situation or completing a task. For example, familiar tasks, repeated exposure, or being in a good mood usually trigger cognitive ease in our "fast" thinking system. Conversely, if we see a situation as novel, problematic, or threatening, we pay more attention and effort. This assessment calls for an increase of systematic thinking or "slow" thinking.

Cognitive ease boosts confidence and saves energy (i.e., "feeling good," "feeling effortless"), but our judgment can be easily misguided by feelings and simple decision rules as a result of cognitive ease (Kahneman, 2011). For example, although "90% fat free" and "10% fat" are identical in describing fat percentage in meat products, the "90% fat free" label tends to evoke stronger positive feelings. Positive feelings are important when we make our purchase decisions. In situations like this, we need a counteracting voice, like "Be careful about the 90% fat free. It actually means 10% fat. Do you still want it after knowing that it has 10% fat?" As you can see in this example, this counteracting voice helps reshape our cognitive landscape from a quick-and-easy thinking to a more systematic thinking.

Cognitive Ease in Communication: Illustrative Examples

Cognitive ease sometimes comes in the form of intuitive preferences and responses to a situation, and they may adversely bias our judgment in favor of certain actions or certain groups over others. In this section, we offer illustrative examples to explain how it occurs. When you read the following cases, think about if you have had similar experiences in your own life.

The first case is from Dr. Shi:

> At our house, if there is any repair work that needs to use hammer and nails, I will write it down and ask my husband to do it. The list can easily get very long before he tackles a single thing on the list. My intuitive reactions are, "You are good at fixing things, so you need to do it. It's lazy to put things off."
>
> Then I think to myself, "Gee, why do I always have to wait for him? Is it that I think handyman work belongs only to men? Does it mean that I cannot handle a hammer and nails?" These thoughts struck me like a light-bulb moment. I felt embarrassed at the thought that I had never even tried to do this work myself; I had simply admitted that I could not do any "handyman's" work.
>
> With this new recognition that I have an automatic association of "handyman" with "men," I decided to test its veracity. My mindset totally shifted from blaming him to wanting to test if I'm able to do repair work. I asked him, "Honey, can you show me where you put the drywall repair kit? I want to try to fix the wall where Oscar (our dog) scratched" The end of this story? I fixed the wall by simply following the instructions on the repair kit. Guess what? This incident opened up a new window to my "handy person" world. I'm actually quite good at repairing things.

Here is another example from Sheryl Sandberg:

> In her TED talk on encouraging more women to lean in and reach for leadership opportunities (Sandberg, 2010), Facebook Chief Operating Officer, Sheryl Sandberg, shared her recent communication experience at work. After Ms. Sandberg gave a speech and went back to her office, a young female employee approached her and mentioned that she continued to take additional questions from the audience after passing a previously-set question limit, and she only took questions from men. What happened was that the female audience members followed the rule ("no more questions should be asked because the question limit has been reached") by putting their hands down. But the male audience members continued to raise questions. Ms. Sandberg continued to address questions from the male audience. She later said, "Obviously I care about this [gender equity], I cannot even notice *that*." (See TED, December 21, 2010, by Sheryl Sandberg)

These examples give rise to two aspects of cognitive ease in communication. First, cognitive ease sometimes comes at the cost of judgmental error, or unintended biased judgment. Many times, such intuitive preferences and reactions are hardly recognizable. Second, it takes reflective thinking effort to recognize that certain underlying preferences influence our behavior in undesired ways (Moskowitz et al., 1999; Wegener et al., 1997). As you read this chapter, you may think of many other forms of bias in addition to gender bias, such as racial or cultural in nature, or one based on communicating differently with someone who has a disability or is a member of a different generation (e.g., boomers versus millennials). With all these examples in mind, let's continue this line of thinking in the next section: conceptualizing interpersonal communication with a new perspective.

A NEW LOOK AT INTERPERSONAL INFLUENCE

In interpersonal communication, managing conflict, influencing others to do things they would not otherwise do, or communicating about biases and biased behaviors are difficult tasks. They can easily lead to feelings of anger and defensiveness (Bosson et al., 2010). Indeed, when we call someone out or correct their biased behavior, we not only run the risk of angering a coworker or friend during such a conversation, we may also be subject to retribution and condemnation as a result of our actions (Czopp et al., 2006; Hyers, 2007; Swim & Hyers, 1999). Given the volatile nature of experiencing and discussing these difficult topics, especially biases and biased behavior, we find rational choice models of communication inadequate for both describing the emotional (and largely unconscious) challenges and for preparing people to become better skilled in such crucial conversations.

Briefly, the rational choice model assumes that people are able to engage in strategic planning and engage in a conversation without the barriers of implicit bias or presumptions (Berger, 1997; Dillard et al., 1989; Shi & Wilson, 2010; Wilson, 2002). At the same time, recent studies and further theoretical development suggest an expansion of rational choice models of communication by including actual human attributes (Burgoon et al., 2000; Cuddy et al., 2008; Fiske & Taylor, 1991; Langer, 1989; Ragins & Winkel, 2011; Shi, 2013).

In this book, we propose an AIM framework (Argumentative Interaction Management) in chapter 2 to address this concern by calling our attention to implicit attitudes and self-other perspective divergence that generate *noises* in our rational thinking. From this point of view, interpersonal influence is seen as an ongoing negotiation of "give-and-take" in terms of what they can do for each other based on a certain collaborative level. Likewise, we approach argumentative interaction as an interpersonal problem that is increasingly solved between people (Czopp & Ashburn-Nardo, 2012).

CHAPTER OVERVIEWS

Before going further, it is a good time for us to offer our readers an overview of this book. In what follows, chapter 2 introduces an AIM framework. It explicates that our own hidden preferences, emotional defenses, and a lack of perspective-taking effort constitute the "noises" and barriers in interpersonal (and relational) communication.

Chapter 3 guides readers through the emotional and behavioral components involved in supportive confrontations. Moving from the theoretical to the practical, we present emotional management and communicative strategies taken from transformative education, team performance, and leadership development. At the heart of these practices is the understanding that we must first confront our own difficult emotions and reactions to challenging situations before we can effectively confront and influence another person's opinions or feelings.

Chapter 4 explores the topics of mindfulness and cognitive effort. In challenging situations, if we spend a little more time in thinking about what we want to say to the other person, could we do a whole lot better in communication? As you will see in the chapter 4, mindfulness can help in only certain areas of communication, not in all. This chapter engages readers to reflect upon our own underlying beliefs about interpersonal communication and rethink about those seemingly mundane daily communication practices regarding the question: "Being mindful about what?"

Chapters 5, 6, and 7 present our research findings on the dynamics of self-other coordination in the contexts of subordinate-to-supervisor upward influence at the workplace (chapter 5), romantic couples' conflict management (chapter 6), and college students' supportive confrontation with others (e.g., giving or taking criticism). As our book transitions from the research findings of AIM framework into managing conversational interventions around biases and biased behavior, we will integrate elements of transformative learning theory into our discussion. Transformative learning theory suggests that when learners have their beliefs and/or identity challenged in the learning environment, they experience a disorienting dilemma, which may initiate other phases of change in their meaning structures (Mezirow, 1994; Mezirow & Taylor, 2009). We argue here that the disorienting dilemma around identity, emotion, and behavior described in transformative learning is key to learning the emotional skills needed to skillfully confront biases and biased behaviors. Said differently, in order to embody the emotional and behavioral skills needed to effectively confront and advise others about biased behaviors, we must first confront our own dysfunctional feelings and emotional defenses.

In summary, this book invites our readers to reflect upon the concept of "communication with ease" from a new perspective. It has two primary purposes: (1) to recognize and reflect upon our intuitive judgment, implicit biases, and automatic thinking in daily communication, and (2) to intervene and improve our everyday conversation when biased communication is likely to occur.

The central message is: What seems apparent and easy can be complicated when it comes to interpersonal communication.

NOTE

1. Pseudonym is used in this case analysis. Pseudonyms are used throughout the rest of the book.

Chapter 2

When Communication Does Not Occur in a Smooth Progression

Xiaowei Shi

ARGUING INVOLVES MORE THAN REASONING

Let's start this chapter with two scenarios about expressing disagreements. The first scenario is about expectations for marriage. My husband and I talked about a close friend's recent divorce. When he shook his head, I could feel the heaviness of this subject and his strong disapproval of divorce. In his mind, being a couple means staying in the relationship forever no matter what. "But what if they have not been happy for the past 20 years? Couples have responsibilities to fulfill each other's needs, especially emotional needs, not just eating together and being there forever! Happiness is very important, you know, it's complicated." I said. I sensed he did not comprehend what I meant by being happy. As you can imagine, we started to argue. We argued back and forth, and emotions flared up in both of us.

The second scenario is about workplace disagreement. During a faculty meeting, our college dean raised a concern that there is a dominant majority in the department, and she suggested that this disparity may have silenced marginalized members. Why did the dean reach this conclusion? We don't know. But upon hearing it, many faculty members were shocked with disbelief. Our impression was that departmental members were strongly supportive of one another; we presumed that everyone felt positive about the department. How could one or more members feel as if they had been silenced? As you can imagine, this instance triggered many colleagues' interests in openly and genuinely discussing practices and procedures of departmental citizenship.

As these examples illustrate, arguing involves exchange of reasons and thoughts between individuals (Hample, 2018). Arguing can take many forms, such as disagreeing with each other (e.g., my husband and me) or presenting viewpoints about "What is/what is not" or "What should be/what should not" as in the case of the dialogue among my departmental colleagues. Such argumentative interactions rarely occur in a smooth progression. Indeed, they contain a series of interactive activities whereby reasoning, supporting, and questioning attempts are interrupted periodically by disagreement-relevant statements.

When we must promote either our own or our group's interests, we face the situation of reasoning with others. Like it or not, we will all face situations like this in our lives. This chapter is about Argumentative Interaction Management (AIM). The AIM framework proposes that there are certain key components in argumentative interactions that individuals must monitor in order to have a comfortable and, perhaps, a smoother arguing experience.

Let's look at some distinct features of argumentative interactions. According to Hample (2018), argumentative interactions are a means of co-creating thoughts socially. This feature suggests that offering and receiving reasons on what to do or how things should work is a natural process of negotiating and shaping the outcome. Depending on how we handle it socially, it could go in different directions and reach constructive or destructive results. This feature points to the important role of monitoring and coordinating during face-to-face argumentative interactions.

Second, argumentative interactions have a persuasion focus. When arguing occurs, it implies that the two parties have differing opinions on certain issues. The primary task of arguing, then, is to encourage the other party to agree with one's own position on an idea or a certain course of action. Therefore, arguing focuses primarily on analyzing the relevance, helpfulness, and legitimacy of a proposed course of action or idea. Arguing serves, at least in part, the purpose of persuading the party to consider and perhaps adopt the proposed position, idea, or course of action.

Third, and finally, there is an intrinsic interdependency between the arguing parties. We choose to argue with another person because the subject under discussion is either vital to the well-being of the relationship or it is significant to the success of a common course of action. In short, we rely on the other party's agreement and participation in order to get something done. Because of this interdependency, when the other party does not comply with what we suggest or have asked for, we feel frustrated. We consider the other party, to a certain extent, has interfered with our relational or task goals. This kind of cognitive appraisal possibly produces a sense of threat, which may easily be accompanied by negative emotions such as anxiety, anger, distress, disappointment, and so on. Keep in mind that these feelings are mutual, meaning that the other party will also have a similar range of cognitive and emotional reactions stemming from the argumentative interactions.

These distinct features of argumentative interactions call for a strategy to manage the tensions embedded in arguing with others in a way that shifts the focal tension from "my way or no way" to something more user-friendly for *both* parties. If both parties hold a combative attitude and seek to gain an upper hand in this argument, then the original nature of reasoning is changed from issues, events, or beliefs into a win-lose competition, with the involved individuals gaining the role of either a "winner" or a "loser." Hence, a "user-friendly" strategy should shift away from combative attitudes by purposely focusing on uncovering the clues that potentially address the issues for mutual benefits. Furthermore, such a strategy needs to cultivate a more positive emotional framework that allows discussion on issues to flow from one party to another in a manner of smooth progression.

In search for such a user-friendly strategy for arguing, this chapter proposes an AIM framework. This framework includes the essential elements of the process of interpersonal influence, and it involves a number of related theories on message production and reception. Moreover, it provides a foundational map for planning and managing argumentative interactions in interpersonal influence.

AIM suggests that, in order to put ourselves into an appropriate emotional framework before and during an argumentative episode, we need to address two communication barriers: (1) the barrier of our own assumptions that we take for granted, and (2) the barrier of gaining a perspective from the other party's point of view. To overcome these barriers, AIM devises a method called "appreciation-oriented alternating inquiries."

You may wonder why we have to pay attention to these many facets. Isn't that cumbersome? Yes, skillful communication entails complicated cognitive planning and tactful execution of verbal and nonverbal expressions. But the good news is that we can acquire such a skill set through everyday communicative interactions and practices. Once we understand its key components, we may gain a potentially powerful tool to handle interpersonal problems, big or small.

This chapter is organized in the following way. To set the stage, it starts with a review of the Goals-Plans-Action (GPA) model to illustrate the process of interpersonal influence. Following this, it lays out the AIM framework and explains how it advances our understanding of interpersonal influence as a coordinated, interactive practice.

GOALS-PLANS-ACTION THEORY

Communication Is Goal-Driven

In communication research, the GPA model represents a contemporary view of how messages are produced (Dillard, 1990, 2004). According to the model, message production is goal-oriented (Wilson, 2002). *Goals* are "future states of affairs" that we want to achieve or maintain during talk to others (Dillard, 2004, p. 185). Researchers note that the number and types of goals individuals seek to address can explain how and why effective and ineffective messages are produced (O'Keefe, 1988). For example, I may have a certain goal in mind when arguing with a person—I want to tell him/her exactly what I think. It's possible that my goal might not be to demonstrate sensitivity or to be convincing. Alternatively, I may have multiple goals: I want to be sensitive to her/his feelings; I don't want to appear nasty or rude; and I want to interest him/her to listen to my ideas.

Dillard, Segrin, and Harden's (1989) research investigated the types of goals that people are aware of and concerned with regarding strategic influence interactions. They found that people want to be persuasive (e.g., "It was very important for me to convince this person"), but they also want to maintain a desirable self-image (e.g., "I was concerned about being true to myself and my values," "I didn't want to look stupid while trying to persuade this person"). People also care about their relational resources (e.g., "I was not willing to risk possible damage to the relationship in order to get what I wanted") and arousal management goals (e.g., "I was afraid of being uncomfortable or nervous").

According to the GPA theory, communication goals motivate and explain our behaviors. Sometimes we say whatever comes to mind, perhaps because that is exactly what we want given the circumstances. Although it appears automatic, it is still oriented toward a particular goal. In other circumstances, we may take more time to choose our words carefully based on their social relevance and possible effects on the target. In such cases, we are aware of the goal assessment process.

Goals motivate plans. Plans are cognitive representations of action sequences intended to help achieve goals (Berger, 1997; Dillard, 2004). Dillard (1990) explained that as the importance of a primary goal increases, so does the willingness to spend more cognitive effort in planning. According to Dillard, planning can be highly deliberative and effortful, relatively effortless, or a mixture of the two. *Heuristic planning* is characterized by its use of simple decision-rules to address one's goals, such as "If she says 'No,' then I will give up." *Deliberative planning* is triggered by the perceptions of inadequacy of the available plans to address goals favorably. In deliberative planning, individuals actively generate plans, fill out incomplete plans, and assess or eliminate alternative plans.

What does deliberative planning look like? My research on how people attempt to persuade their organizational leaders for work improvement provides some insights (Shi, 2013). Using a thought-listing procedure, I found that deliberate planning involves at least four components: (1) situation assessing thoughts (e.g., what is going on in this situation), (2) goal assessing thoughts (e.g., what I want to say and achieve in this conversation), (3) caution thoughts in anticipating possible difficulties or obstacles (e.g., what if he or she does not like this idea), and (4) alternative action thoughts (e.g., what would be other options if I don't talk to him or her directly).

After planning, messages exit to the real world. One consistent finding across multiple studies is that goals influence a message's features in distinct and predictable ways (Dillard et al., 1989; Shi, 2013). For example, a persuasion goal has a significant positive association with the amount of reasoning presented in messages. On the other hand, the goals of conversation management and relationship maintenance are associated with different positivity features in that message, such as expressions of approval, ingratiation, respect, or gratitude. As such, one important lesson we have learned from this line of research is that our cognitive landscape (e.g., goals and plans) matters in determining our communication qualities.

SOCIAL INTERACTION THEORY

The GPA model is a prominent theoretical perspective on strategic communication in our discipline. As noted earlier, it focuses on goal formation and multi-level planning (e.g., context assessment and caution thought). To provide us a broader perspective on the dynamics in social exchanges, let's look at another theoretical framework: the Social Interaction Theory proposed by psychologist Robert Freed Bales (1970, 1999).

In his Social Interaction Theory, Bales suggested that social interactions need to be examined along three dimensions: (1) a social actor's task-oriented motives versus emotion expressive motives, (2) an individual's propensity for dominance versus submissiveness on decision-making, and (3) his or her friendliness versus unfriendliness in coordination of actions with others. As individuals' have different orientations along these three dimensions, conflict is almost inevitable in all social interactions. As Bales explained, even within ourselves, we sometimes have conflicting needs and goals: for example, not only wanting to gain the upper hand but also wanting to be friendly and agreeable in dispute situations.

Social Interaction Theory highlights the complexity in mutual influence system, in which actions generate reactions, instrumental goals interlock with emotional expressions, and current actions leave consequences for future events. You may wonder, "Now I know that these three-dimensional factors are involved in a space for conflict, what should I do in an interaction if I want to manage disagreement more effectively?" Based on three decades of observational and laboratory studies, Bales and his associates found that the process (or "time trajectory") of how we *build* the interaction space will significantly influence the interaction outcomes. Researchers found that how we talk with each other generates changes (or so-called "the field effect"), and changes build a new motion of change for future interaction dynamics. For example, if one is willing to listen to other's feedback, the field effect of "liking" will increase, and in turn, it will change the motion of how one is likely to influence the other's behavior.

According to Bales, strategic actors need to monitor all the important parts of an interaction (e.g., task, emotion, and dominance) and gather information about what is going on in the field, such as barriers and obstacles. As a parsimonious theoretical framework, the Social Interaction Theory provides a valuable method for observing and diagnosing the key components in a social interaction system and their functions on a multi-dimensional scale (Bales, 1999; Hare, 2000).

As the following discussion will illustrate, AIM framework in this book shares a similar line of thinking proposed in the Social Interaction Theory, recognizing the hidden or nonobvious effect of self-monitoring and inquiring actions on eliciting attraction and cooperative interests from the other party. On the other hand, however, AIM distinguishes itself from previous theories (both GPA and Social Interaction Theory) by focusing on communicative *meanings* created and shared during interpersonal, problem-solving interactions.

AIM is about finding the meanings we automatically attach to our message choices and the meanings of other party's messages. In a more nuanced way, AIM framework reminds us that the meanings we attempt to communicate with each other are more than words. Rather, implicit biases and presumptions also come into play in influencing how we choose to interact with others.

WHAT ELSE DO WE NEED TO KNOW?

Contemporary research on interpersonal influence is based on a rational-choice model, assuming that people are able to engage in strategic planning and participate in a conversation without barriers of implicit bias or presumptions. However, more empirical evidence and theoretical development stimulate a need to expand the rational-choice model by considering actual human attributes (Burgoon et al., 2000; Cuddy et al., 2008, 2006; Fiske & Taylor, 1991; Langer, 1989; Ragins & Winkel, 2011; Shi, 2013). Two relevant human attributes are noteworthy: (1) rather than being bias-free, human minds have implicit biases and hidden preferences (or "blind spots," Banaji & Greenwald, 2013) on a variety of subjects, and they potentially generate *noises* in rational thinking; and (2) rather than being easy, it is difficult for human minds to gain perspectives from the other's points of view (or "self-other overlap"). These attributes are particularly important in message production because they help explain why communicators sometimes produce less-than-optimal messages, even hurtful messages.

To account for our everyday message production processes that are more automatic and less rational, a revised framework is called for. This framework not only recognizes our cognitive limitations but also features a built-in mechanism to improve mutual understanding in interactions. With these viewpoints in mind, an AIM framework is laid out next.

THE AIM FRAMEWORK

The AIM framework is an extension of the GPA model. Two fundamental assumptions about interpersonal communication inspired the development of the AIM framework.

The first assumption is that we are capable of monitoring and modifying our communication behavior. There is more than one way to exert influence in communication. The outcome of influence varies depending on how we act during argumentative episodes. If one way does not work, we can change and try a new way to communicate.

For example, a few years ago, I conducted a research project called "What if you could redo?" (see chapter 6). In this project, I asked participants to recall a conflict situation in which they had said and done something that ended up hurting the relationship very badly. Next, I asked, "If you could turn back the clock, how would you redo this conflict interaction to make it the most positive experience for you and your partner?" To my surprise, almost all participants expressed an alternative approach to handling the conflict. Put differently, they wanted to modulate themselves in a way that would make their communication with their romantic partners more pleasant and effective. Naturally, I pondered "Why didn't they do that in the first place?" "What prevented them from doing the more effective communication in the first place?"

The second assumption is that communication is a coordinated action. That is, a skillful communicator needs to consider his or her own resources, the characteristics and power of the other party, the management of emotions and symbolic meanings that a message carries, and then choose certain strategies that will motivate the other to contemplate and/or adopt a proposed idea (Shi & Wilson, 2017). As we can see from this description, a sender's message shapes the receiver's perceptions and preferences, stimulating a certain level of either willingness or reluctance to collaboration. From this point of view, interpersonal influence is not something that one does to the other. Rather, it is seen as an ongoing negotiation of "give-and-take" in terms of what they can do for each other based on a certain collaborative level. From this point of view, what seems to be an impasse in arguing may be the beginning of a new understanding of the problem under discussion, or it may generate a new route for discussion. Therefore, gaining perspectives and motivating joint problem-solving effort are crucial parts in managing difficult communication encounters.

RECOGNIZING BIASED THINKING

There is one factor that is too often ignored in strategic communication research. That is, we all have "blind spots" (Banaji & Greenwald, 2013) in our thinking, which may explain why we sometimes miscalculate a situation and miscommunicate with the other party. Rather than assuming people are rational communicators, the present AIM framework includes the factor of "implicit attitudes awareness" in addition to goal formation and plan generation in message production. It suggests that implicit attitudes (or biases) and some sort of taken-for-granted responses tend to sustain and fuel a "chaotic" argumentative interaction.

Our Latent Mindset

To describe what our latent mindset is, let's think about the following example. Imagine how individuals' implicit attitudes (or IA) toward decision-making affect their communication in this case. Person A prefers easygoing decision-making, holding a mindset of "Don't think too much. Pick the easiest way. Then chill." In contrast, person B finds it unbearable to adopt such an approach to decision-making, believing that "the easiest way can rarely be the best way. Why not try a little harder?" When A and B have to make a joint decision, it's likely they will demonstrate clashing views.

A personal example is that I found it annoying (and somewhat amusing) when my husband insisted on buying the biggest and/or the cheapest TV. For him, the decision-making for a major purchase should follow a simple, heuristic rule—the biggest TV with the lowest price would be the best choice. I could not agree. I ask myself, "Do simple decisions always mean bad decisions?" In my mind, I automatically associate rational decision-making (e.g., systematic examination, sometimes with excruciating effort) with better results. Asking such an evaluative question usually prompts me to reflect upon my own latent perceptions and realize that I could be wrong, and he may be right.

The term "implicit attitudes" (IA) refers to the mental process whereby an individual's underlying preferences or hidden beliefs exert influence on judgment and current action by means of bypassing conscious awareness (Greenwald & Banaji, 2017). Ironically, researchers find that many of our IA are the ones that we would explicitly reject if we had a chance to think more carefully. In their research, Banaji and Greenwald (2013) reported that, among the 1.5 million white Americans who participated in the online Implicit Attitudes Test (IAT), 40% of them describe themselves as egalitarian and hold explicit beliefs of race equality. In other words, they support equality and are willing to put these ideals into practice out of conscious choice. But they nonetheless demonstrated an "automatic white preference" mindset in the Race IAT result, in which they are more likely to associate Caucasians with American citizens, associate Asian Americans with foreigners, and are more ready to offer help to white than to black individuals.

As this point, you may wonder: What if we are able to recognize those hidden preferences and IA, would we make better judgments when interacting with our significant others, our neighbors, our friends, or colleagues?

How to Recognize Biased Communication?

In communication, during the goal formation stage, the communicator who sends a message identifies socially significant characteristics in the communication target (e.g., gender, race, and occupational position) and uses those cues to form IA that enact subsequent behavior (Hogg & Terry, 2000). As such, an automatic thinking mode on how to talk and what responses to get from a certain communication partner plays an influential role in the goal formation stage of communication interaction.

The Action Assembly Theory (Greene, 1997) offers insights on how messages with our personal preferences and hidden attitudes are generated in everyday communication. Greene (1997) explains that when people encounter a situation, a relevant set of procedural records (thought units) can be activated. Once activated, these thought units need to find ways to integrate with each other in order to form a meaningful utterance. Such a process can be chaotic, dynamic, or quite automatic.

One way to assemble thoughts and produce messages is to rely on our existing cognitive schemas. Here is an example to illustrate the relationship of our cognitive schemas between a "professor" and a "male" prototype. Pay attention to the automatic assembly process in associating "he" with "Dr." in this case. When I was studying at Purdue University, one professor talked to us about her "female professor" burden. She insisted her students should call her "Dr. Snyder" instead of her first name "Suzan." Both she and her husband taught in our department, and both held doctorate degrees. But from the first days of their joining the department, students would invariably call her "Suzan" and her husband "Dr. Snyder." "Why not the other way around?" she asked us. Why don't students call her "Dr. Snyder," and address her husband as "Gerald"? (Gerald Snyder and Suzan Snyder are both pseudonyms).

While listening to her explanation of her experience as a female professor, I thought to myself, "Wow, that is true! Why do I feel compelled to call her Suzan, whereas I always call her husband Dr. Snyder?" I felt terrible about my bias. Until that moment, my fellow classmates and I did not realize that our implicit addressing of our beloved professors contributed to the perpetuation of gender-related biases in academia. If we knew, we would never do it. What was going on in our mind?

Getting this "shivering alert" was helpful for me to recognize and confirm my biased thinking in favor of associating a male figure with a doctoral title. Starting from that moment, I now always pay attention to how I address female professors, female colleagues, female officers, or female sales representatives. I make sure to use their professional titles when I speak to them, regardless of their gender roles.

The previous example illustrates three aspects of how to recognize our implicit biases. First, we need to take a break from our automatic thinking mode. During our initial encounter in a communication situation, our cognitive responses may involve an array of situationally relevant thoughts we seek to assemble in order to produce a message. During this stage, our hidden beliefs, implicit biases, and preferences come into play. My own study (2013) found that roughly 10% of our cognitive responses in this stage relate to "caution thoughts." Such thoughts anticipate obstacles and barriers in communication. For example, "What if she or he does not like me to call her Suzan?" and "What if saying so will offend her or him?" In a small amount of our thinking, this kind of caution thoughts may help us break the automatic responses in favor of certain subtle forms of biased communication.

Second, we need to ask questions about the other party's wants and needs rather than assuming we can read someone's mind. In this regard, Banaji and Greenwald (2013) presented a "no-brainer" solution. Instead of making assumptions, we can start a conversation by asking the other party a question. For example, "What do you prefer to be addressed?" or "I wonder what are the ways in which you might like to change and what you would want me to change next time when we start to argue?" Such questions signal our interest in acknowledging input from the other party. They also help avoid generating those automatic, potentially biased messages.

Third, and finally, debiasing requires creative thinking. To counteract our automatic ways of "assembling" certain thoughts in response to a situation, we need to try some novel ways of engaging in a conversation. The underlying goal is to leave it open for interpretations rather than categorizing it automatically as what it is.

Consider this quick example. When my daughter was 5 years old, she asked me a question about my habit of eating with chopsticks. It struck me as a novel way to talk about my cultural heritage and my association of eating and physical endurance. She asked me, "Mama, you always pick your food from those plates, put it in your bowl, then eat. Is it exhausting for your arm? Do you feel tired to do this many times during a meal?"

Her question offered an utterly new perspective for me to see my eating habits. The way I eat is by picking food from a big serving platter, and this style is implicitly associated with my Chinese heritage, which I take for granted. But my daughter asked about the physical endurance in association with eating in this manner. Thanks to her novel question, I chose to change my habits. Now, I gather food all at once from platters and eat from my plate, never making multiple trips.

GAINING PERSPECTIVES

In addition to IA awareness, perspective-taking (PT) is another cognitive mechanism that influences communication interaction. By definition, perspective-taking refers to our mental process of imagining ourselves in another's shoes (Galinsky et al., 2005). When arguing, we can respond by relying on our own perceptions. Such instant response without much thinking is called reactive communication. On the other hand, we can inhibit the impulse to react by trying to gather information from the other party's point of view. The AIM framework proposes that the willingness and ability to think from another's point of view (or developing a self-other overlap) will contribute to greater collaboration in argumentative talk.

Self-Other Overlapping Is Cognitively Demanding

During arguing episodes, we want to understand where one is coming from, what we might call the "why" question. Problematic Integration theory (hereafter called PI) suggests that gaining perspective from the other party during arguing can be particularly challenging (Babrow, 1992, 1995, 2001). According to PI theory, each individual develops his or her own probabilistic and evaluative orientations, and they typically arise and blend or "integrate" with little conscious thought in shaping our outlook and action. Two individuals may hold diverging expectations and desires as they enter a conversation. As a conversation unfolds, communication is the primary medium, source, and resource in PI experiences (Babrow, 1992). In other words, PI is, at once, both an individual psychological process and an inherently communicative phenomenon.

How Do I Get the Other's Perspective?

According to PI theory, interpersonal communication can transform divergence by, for example, encouraging reappraisals of probability and value, seeking common ground, and recasting my view and your view as complementary. Although these transformations may bring relief from the original divergence, these new orientations themselves can be problematic, thus prompting an ongoing search for meaning.

Building upon PI theory, AIM suggests that it is necessary to gauge the other party's meaning-making process in order to make arguments that are more context specific, such as acknowledging and addressing the other person's unique "probabilistic" and "evaluative" orientations on a subject matter. When gaining perspective from the other party, AIM suggests that we need to seek for answers to questions such as, "Could you share with me, from your point of view, what caused the current disagreement?" or "In your mind, what are the consequences of us being in the current state?" By gathering these pieces of information from the other party, we know more about the needs, concerns, and motives in his or her mind. Such questions also help us form context-specific goals and plans on what to say and how to respond in subsequent interactions.

APPRECIATION-ORIENTED INQUIRIES AS ALTERNATING FORCE

So far, we may feel that interpersonal arguing is mostly a matter of managing the barriers of our own hidden attitudes and the challenges that may overshadow us when we hope for a smooth exchange of ideas. But other factors may take a toll on argumentative progression as well, such as emotional burdens and a decreased attraction to the other because of arguing.

Rather than getting one's way or maximizing one's turn to talk, AIM devises a counterintuitive approach for managing argumentative interaction. That is, to use appreciation-oriented inquiries to alternate the communication process, giving the floor to the other party, and hence motivating a joint effort to deal with the issue at hand.

Consistent with the GPA perspective, AIM framework highlights how individuals' inner thoughts influence emotions and responses to other's messages. From an AIM's perspective, "getting one's way" should not be an ultimate goal for conflict resolution. Rather, being willing to modify one's expectations as new information or unanticipated changes emerge should be part of one's strategic goals. In addition, being able to find clues that reveal the other party's unexpressed concerns and to address those concerns counts as an important goal in conflict talk. From this perspective, argumentative interaction is a process of "mutual modification."

For example, a wife suggests that they attend a classical piano concert to celebrate their 10th-year wedding anniversary, but the husband says, "I don't want to go." It turns out that the husband does not want to wear a tuxedo or anything formal. He does not think it is romantic and fun for them to sit there for two hours listening to music without talking with his wife. He wants something more casual and intimate. Through discussions, the couple decides to attend a wine-tasting event and have dinner together at a beautiful vineyard. As this example illustrates, mutual modification in conflict communication involves not only modifying the other party in order to achieve one's agenda but also being open to make adjustments (or "be modified") as conversations unfold over time.

The "inquiry-oriented alternating communication" is a key to mutual modification. It suggests that communicators should seek to adopt an appreciative mindset, to value the other party's input, in addition to their attempt to reason with others on what one thinks is "right" or "should be." This method involves a two-step procedure when responding to a provocative comment in conflict situations. First, to monitor one's automatic thinking and reactions, telling oneself "Oh, wait! What is the 'real' underlying concern or hidden meaning in her/his message?" Second, to express an interest in understanding what the actual intention is in the message. For example, asking a clarification question or acknowledging the legitimacy of that comment, saying, "You made a good point."

The Emotional Factor

Remember the reciprocity feature of argumentative interactions. If we feel we are emotionally running high, it is very likely that our counterpart will feel the same. Therefore, one of the essential tasks in the AIM framework is to manage our emotional and cognitive landscape when we are disagreeing with others.

Our emotional experience and cognitive appraisal are deeply interrelated. It is the cognitive appraisal of a triggering situation (not the situation itself) that determines how we experience emotion (Clark & Beck, 2010). People's responses to a potential threat involve two stages: (1) primary cognitive appraisal that involves a primitive, automatic state of alarm, and (2) a secondary, more elaborative reappraisal that involves assessments of one's coping abilities and situational cues. Depending on the quality of this cognitive assessing process, we will either end up in an uncontrollable emotional outburst or a non-anxious state of worry. The latter state of emotion tends to motivate a person to take actions toward problem-solving, which is the desirable state that we aim to maintain during argumentative interactions.

How do we make our emotions stay cool at a non-anxious level during a heated episode of discussion? Research shows that cognitive reappraisal serves this purpose. Reappraisal seeks to re-evaluate the meaning of an emotionally charged event. In studying anxiety management, my colleagues and I found that our own self-talk influences our emotional feelings (Shi et al., 2013, 2017). In particular, our negative self-talk is associated with a heightened level of emotional turmoil. Therefore, an appraisal effort involves redirecting our negative cognition to neutral emotions. For example, instead of thinking, "This idea sounds so absurd" or "How dare you talk to me like that," redirect the inner thinking to further inquiries, "It appeared bizarre, it was rude in manner, but did he or she make an interesting point?" Such cognitive reappraisals help shift our emotion from primitive, automatic reactions to more complex feelings, such as hopefulness, authentic interest, or curiosity.

The Inquiry Factor: A Driving Force for Alternating Communication Process

So far, this chapter provides all these sections to make the point that communicators need to be open to alter one's original plan (with recognition of one's implicit biases) to meet the other's needs during a disagreement. Through mutual modification, as conversation unfolds, we can move the communication process toward problem-solving. One distinct feature in the AIM framework is its emphasis on using appreciation-orientated inquiries to motivate and engage the other party in a conversation. Arguing can be both cognitively demanding and emotionally draining. What kind of mechanism will drive this course of action toward a more fruitful direction? AIM framework proposes that appreciation-focused alternating actions may serve this purpose.

Alternating in communication emphasizes using appreciation-oriented inquiries to get input from the other party. The key function of alternating in communication is to give opportunities to both parties to express ideas that are intrinsic to a high-quality problem-solving, while signaling interest and appreciation. For example, inquiries such as, "Your idea is so new to me. Why is that relevant to this topic?" or "I'm interested in knowing what is on your mind" allow the other party to expand on his or her viewpoint. The notions of "new idea" or "I'm interested" not only signal appreciation but also express shared interests and attraction, and these affirmations motivate the other party to contribute. Such expressions also give each party a chance to negotiate, withdraw, resume, or move forward on a subject in more detail.

Alternating Motion and Better-Than-Rational Outcome

The concept of alternating process in communication derives from collective problem-solving literature. In collective problem-solving research, Nobel Prize laureate and political economist Elinor Ostrom's findings are noteworthy. Ostrom (1998) challenged the conventional wisdom that public goods, such as fishing ponds, woods, and pollution control, will be overexploited in the long run. The rationale is because public resources are shared, individuals may want to maximize their own short-term self-interest, but such seemingly rational decisions can produce outcomes that leave all participants worse off in the long run.

Contrary to what conventional wisdom suggests, Ostrom's field observations (1998) revealed that public goods can be used in a way that is economically and environmentally sustainable without external interventions. According to Ostrom, through frequent face-to-face communication among community members, norms of trust, reputation, and reciprocity are developed; rules are negotiated to determine how best to take care of the common goods. The outcome of such collective actions is considered better than individuals' rational choice.

AIM framework proposes that alternating behavior during argumentative interactions can serve a similar function. By seeking and offering new ideas, the appreciation-oriented alternating behavior signals mutual support and willingness for joint problem-solving. As this alternating process unfolds, communicators can build trust and possibly attraction with each other. Such alternating processes in seeking inputs may provide opportunities to achieve a better outcome than individuals' rational choice in "getting one's way."

AIM FRAMEWORK: A CHAIN OF INTERACTIONS

This section offers a brief explanation of how AIM operates. The process is depicted in figure 2.1. Let's assume there are two parties in a communicative interaction ("you" and "me"). Depending on our initial levels of IA awareness and effort in GP in the dyads, a conversation engagement can begin with a relatively low, moderate, or high level of willingness to collaborate with each other through arguing and reasoning.

To achieve a relatively smooth and productive interpersonal communication experience, one or both communicators (again, "you" and "me") are suggested by the AIM framework to adopt an alternating approach to coordinate the communication process. That is, reasoning and appreciation-oriented inquiries need to go hand in hand with each other in an alternating process. In essence, alternating communication process suggests communicators gain an understanding of the other's point of view by explicitly inviting input while upholding the alternating turn for the other party to speak.

During this process, each communicator's goals and plans are monitored, revised, improved, or repaired. The purpose of purposely establishing an alternating dynamic in AIM is to improve the level of collaboration. Through

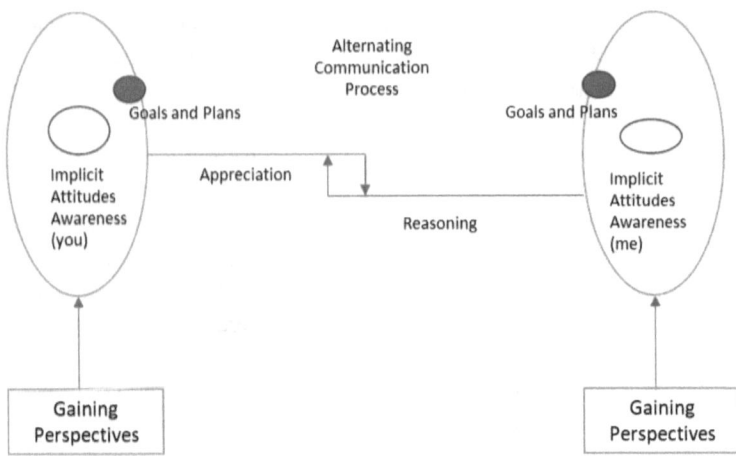

Figure 2.1. The Core Components and Relationships in Argumentative Interaction Management (AIM).

giving and receiving issue-relevant ideas, AIM suggests that "you" and "I" are working on problem-solving as well as settling on a social meaning that is co-created and mutually agreed, no matter if it is about the procedure or how you should properly treat each other. Put differently, the actions taken during the alternating process in communication create norms and an atmosphere for smooth progression in argumentative interactions.

AIM framework is distinct from the GPA model in three ways. First, it highlights the two-way interaction, embracing the "I see you" and "you see me" dynamics. The alternating flow is depicted as two "arms" reaching out from each side, emphasizing the active roles of appreciation-oriented inquiries and reasoning in creating a collaborative level between the two parties. Second, the AIM framework reminds us to recognize our own limits (e.g., implicit biases, hidden preferences) when talking to others. Third, and finally, it emphasizes that the foundation for effective communication is built upon GPs from each other, from which goals and plans are devised and implemented. For this reason, the "gaining perspectives" factor is depicted in figure 2.1 as a base, from where "you" and "me" can face each other to communicate.

LOOKING AHEAD

In the remainder of this book, each chapter will specially address one process around this framework, such as IA awareness, effort in GP, and skillful confrontations to engage in dialogues in difficult situations. Before leaving this chapter, I challenge you to think about the concept of *ease* in communication.

What Is *Ease* in Communication?

As mentioned, we need to manage argumentative interactions with our significant others in big and small life situations. All of us face uncertainties in light of confrontational communication encounters. The above discussion of the AIM framework seems to imply the following features that help cultivate a sense of *ease* in complex communication situations: (1) *elaboration* in the sense of elaborating on plans about how to act in a conversation, (2) *awareness* in the sense of examining one's own attitudes and acknowledging what the other party needs and wants, (3) *smooth* exchange of ideas by adopting an alternating approach to seek inputs, and (4) *effectiveness* in the sense of focusing on the issues at hand and not on the person. The initials of these four features are EASE.

You may question that this kind of "ease" in the AIM framework implies effort rather than a lack of effort. Yes, it takes more time and effort to monitor and modulate our communication with others compared to saying whatever is on the top of our head. But the extra effort results in a reward in the long run. We sustain a relationship with our significant others, gain new insights from each other's point of view, and potentially garner an outcome that is better than our individual's separate effort. From this perspective, ease and effort in communication are deeply interrelated. To a certain extent, they are one, corroborating each other.

Chapter 3

Identifying and Meeting the Emotional Challenges of Supportive Confrontation

Steve Mortenson

Consider the following scenarios for an interpersonal intervention. Working under an intense timeline, Tamara, a young woman of color, has just finished giving an excellent presentation to her team when Kyle (an older white man) comes up afterward.

Kyle: That was really good, Tamara! You are so well spoken. It's so great to see a young gal show that kind of poise under pressure.
    Tamara gives a strained smile and nods. Janice, the team leader, also hears Kyle's remarks. She has been told the same thing countless times and she's had enough. She pulls Kyle aside:
Janice: Kyle, do you have any idea how racist and sexist it was to say that to Tamara? Telling her she's well spoken? She's got a degree from Northwestern—how do you expect her to talk?!
Kyle: (taken aback) What are you talking about? I just told her she did a great job! How's that racist or sexist? I was complimenting her on her work!
Janice: You called her a *young gal*—that's demeaning.
Kyle: She *is* a young gal, she's just out of college! Look, Janice, I'll tell you what's demeaning: supporting a colleague's work and then being called racist for it.

That got out of hand pretty fast; tempers flared and very little was accomplished.
    Consider an alternative:
    After Tamara's presentation, Janice can feel how angry she is over Kyle's remarks. She goes to her office realizing her anger in the moment is driven by pain from her own past experiences of racial and sexual discrimination. She takes a few minutes to separate her feelings about the past from the needs of the present

situation. When she feels clearer, she decides on her goals for confronting Kyle about his behavior. When she's clear on that, she calls him in to speak to her.

> *Janice*: Hi, Kyle, I wanted to talk with you about something—and let me say up front that I know you value the women you work with, and I know that when you compliment Tamara on her presentation in the meeting, you're sincere in what you say—you'd never say anything to demean her. But there are two things you need to be aware of: When a black person hears that he or she is "well spoken," what that person hears is "*you* are well spoken, *unlike* most black people." So, you can imagine, this is not something that makes Tamara feel good about herself or what she did. A much better compliment for a good presentation is to be told you were *eloquent* or *insightful*.
>
> Also, when we attach someone's youth or gender to her accomplishments, it actually diminishes the person. It sets her apart from the standard instead of holding her up as the standard.
>
> It might surprise us that that a young woman like Tamara can present her ideas with such authority, but surprise at her skill doesn't help her any; it can actually cast doubts about her ability. I know you don't want that either, so may I show you this video on implicit bias? I think it will make clear what I mean, and I think you'll be glad you saw it—I know I was. I was really shocked to see some of the biases I had. I had no idea how easy it is to fall into bias and hurt someone else without even realizing it. This video really made these subtle forms of bias more understandable for me. Would you like to watch it?

Kyle is a little surprised—but he agrees to sit down and watch the video with Janice. Afterward they have a civil and productive discussion.

As you can see, discussing and, in particular, correcting others' biased behavior is a delicate business. In the second scenario, Janice employs what I call *Supportive Confrontation*. When Janice effectively confronts Kyle, she remains supportive of him while critiquing his behavior, shows him the ramifications of what he said and offers him a solution.

For example, at the very onset, Janice makes sure to protect Kyle's self-image or *Face*, during their encounter. Face theorists argue that receiving advice or correction calls into question the recipient's sense of value and competence, and it limits the autonomy and range of their future behavior (Feng, 2014; Goldsmith & MacGeorge, 2000). Likewise, giving advice threatens face when recipients perceive advice as "butting in" and constraining autonomy and when people interpret advice as or corrections implying ignorance or incompetence (Goldsmith, 1999, 2000). Janice avoided these pitfalls by supporting Kyle's intentions and sense of self while critiquing the execution of his unfortunate compliment.

Even more critical to her success, before she confronts Kyle, Janice does some focused mental and emotional work to identify and separate her own past traumas with sexual discrimination from her emotions about the present situation. As recipients of gender discrimination themselves, women confronting sexism face the added challenge of managing feelings regarding their own past experiences of discrimination (Mortenson, 2017). Experiencing sexist behavior can leave recipients with intense feelings of anger and depression-related emotions that can last for weeks after the initial event (Bosson, Pinel, & Vandello, 2010). Moreover, the type of subtle or implicit bias that Kyle was embodying with his condescending compliment typically leaves women with fewer resources or strategies for coping and responding to discrimination (Good & Rudman, 2010).

When we are unable to discuss, cope, or otherwise express emotional pain, we hold onto these painful feelings and develop an *emotional charge* around the suppressed pain (Richo, 2008). This emotional charge can be triggered by events or people that recall our original suppressed pain, and it adds to the cognitive and emotional effort needed to deal with our feelings in the present moment (Hollis, 2008). Having dealt with her own pain consciously, Janice is able to better manage her own feelings and offer advice more skillfully to Kyle.

It is also important to note that Kyle truly had no idea he was insulting one of his coworkers. One of the biggest challenges to managing our own implicit biases is that our biases are largely unconscious, outside of our control, and associated with feelings of fear, anxiety, and discomfort (Staats, 2014; Fazio et al., 1995; Dovidio et al., 1997). We are all susceptible to implicit biases (Rutland et al., 2005); as children, we develop biased associations from our authority figures, observing others, and the media (Castelli, Zogmaister, & Tomelleri, 2009; Dasgupta, 2013; Kang, 2012). Surprisingly, our implicit biases often stand in direct contradiction to those beliefs we consciously hold and endorse (Greenwald & Krieger, 2006; Reskin, 2005). What this means is that although we may consciously espouse and strive for goals such as equity and inclusion for all people, we may still unconsciously fall into biased thoughts and discriminatory behaviors, often through fear and anxiety. Understanding that fear is a primary emotional context behind implicit bias is crucial to effectively managing our biases and helping others with theirs. This chapter is dedicated to examining some of the emotional obstacles that prevent us from effectively confronting other people about volatile topics and we offer some initial strategies for overcoming them.

With all this in mind, I will start this chapter by describing in detail four emotional obstacles that prevent effective communication, especially when confronting other people or helping them confront their problems: (1) Recognizing the emotional disconnect between knowing what to say and do—but not actually saying and doing it. (2) Identifying some of the unconscious sources of our reactive and dysfunctional feelings. (3) Managing and preventing the intrusion of past fears, griefs, and traumas onto present situations and people. (4) Defusing the emotional-interpersonal dynamics that drive much of our dysfunctional communication.

Next, I will discuss the theory and rationale behind what I call the Strengths and Shadows Deep Personality Assessment as a method of raising our emotional awareness. The deep assessment is the first part of a fourfold intervention of *Supportive Confrontation* designed to help people communicate skillfully during tense or challenging communication. I have taught these supportive confrontation interventions to students in leadership programs, to athletic teams, and to professional administrators, environmental engineers, nurses, psychiatrists, and physicians. I will discuss how the deep assessment reflects elements of transformative learning theory's "disorienting dilemma" and describe the intervention's final goal: skillful and supportive confrontation. Let's turn to our first emotional obstacle, the difference between knowing what to do or say but not actually engaging in skillful communication.

THE EMOTIONAL OBSTACLES TO SUPPORTIVE CONFRONTATION

Emotional Obstacle 1: The Emotional Disconnect between Knowing and Doing

One problem that we all face in any confrontation is emotion: whether we are confronting some aspect of our own personality, another person's problematic behavior, or helping someone else confront a problem of their own, we must first face our own emotions. Our problem is that certain things, situations, and people simply "set us off." When we are set off, we are rendered ineffective; even when we know the right words and messages to use, we are not motivated to say them.

I found a good example of this disconnect by studying emotional support and comforting. When we provide emotional support to another person in crisis, we are helping them confront their problem or calamity and, in a very real sense, we are confronting their problem and their emotional distress. It is no surprise then, that many people are fearful about comforting others; they worry about being "sucked in" to another's problems, fear having to witness strong displays of sadness or rage, and are anxious about "saying the wrong things" and "making things worse" (Burleson, Albrecht, & Saranson, 1994).

Despite such fears, people across different national cultures and languages (i.e., America and China) generally recognize and agree on what constitutes the most sensitive and effective things to say and do when someone is upset. Specifically, both our Chinese and American participants rated support messages designed to validate the target person's upset feelings, provide ego support, and give perspective and advice as to the most skillful (Burleson & Mortenson, 2003). Yet, even with a cross-cultural consensus on what works best, we found that people differed significantly in the importance they put on pursuing different kinds of support goals. As we've seen, pursuing different goals can lead to effective or ineffective behaviors. For example, emotion-focused support goals (wanting to make the person feel better) and problem-focused support goals (wanting to help them solve their dilemma) are associated with effective and helpful social support behaviors. In contrast, emotion-avoidant support goals (seeking to distract the person or minimize their feelings or problem) led to unhelpful and dysfunctional social support behaviors (Barbee, Lawrence, & Cunningham, 1998).

We found that while Americans viewed emotion-focused goals as the most important to pursue, Chinese participants saw problem-focused and emotion-avoidant goals as the most important to pursue. Given these findings, we argued that the recognition of effective support messages represents a kind of *emotional appropriateness* while pursuing specific kinds of support goals better represents a sense of *emotional efficacy* (Mortenson et al., 2006).

In the same study, we also found that individual (rather than cultural) differences drove the preference for emotion- and problem-focused goals over emotion-avoidant goals in both cultures. The difference that made a difference in pursuing effective support was how much individuals identified with *both* a valued sense of individual distinction (i.e., being recognized for valued talents or characteristics) and a sense of interpersonal belonging (i.e., feeling emotionally connected to other people). In short, effectively helping another person confront his or her troubles and calamities begins with how we feel about ourselves and our connection to others. I also found the same pattern for people confronting their own problems. Across both Chinese and American cultures, people who had greater levels of social skill and interpersonal trust in others were also more likely to seek social support and make others aware of their needs in culturally effective ways (Mortenson, 2009).

So, if feeling the right way about ourselves, the person, and the situation is key, how do we get there? How do we learn to recognize the fears and emotional patterns that derail our ability to skillfully confront challenging situations and people? I have found the best place to start is by looking into the unconscious side of the personality, the psychological shadow. By exploring the material we carry in our psychological shadows, we can begin to understand the things that make us reactive and unskillful (Mortenson, 2007).

Emotional Obstacle 2: The Psychological Shadow

Briefly stated, Carl Jung and his students conceived of the personality as having both a conscious side that includes all the things about ourselves we are aware of and admit to and an unconscious, shadow side that includes desires, feelings, and behaviors that we deny in ourselves through our refusal to acknowledge them. Such denied traits are usually seen by our authority figures and community as inferior or immoral ways to feel, think, and behave (Jung, Campbell, & Hull, 1971; Moore & Gillette, 1991).

The formation of an individual's psychological shadow is a natural process that occurs during childhood: a child's shadow functions to hold all the socially risky parts of their personality outside of their awareness. In this way, the shadow helps us to adapt and better fit into our families and communities and to better identify with the values encouraged by our authority figures and role models (Hollis, 2008).

The price for our adaptation during childhood is that we often leave important talents and personality traits underdeveloped and unexpressed. For example, people who were raised to be helpful and altruistic often have a difficult time saying "no" when asked for a favor they would rather refuse. Moreover, altruistic people often find it difficult to ask for help themselves no matter how much they need it. Because they have put their ability to hold boundaries and act upon their own needs for assistance into shadow, when those needs arise, unconscious feelings of fear and shame are triggered. While this shadow helped them better identify with the altruistic values of their childhood, the inability to set boundaries and effectively protect their own time and energy makes adulthood more difficult (Johnson, 1993; Jung, 1969).

One important shadow dynamic related to discussing issues of bias is what Gillette and Moore (1991) call the victim/perpetrator shadow. Put simply, we deny our perpetrator to convince ourselves (and others) that we are kinder and more moral and ethical than we actually are. We claim to be innocent and unaccountable despite the facts or feelings of others; we often play the victim to shield ourselves from blame or responsibility for bad outcomes. We deny our victim in order to suppress painful memories of feeling powerless and abused. We will downplay moments of abuse as "not that bad" or "they meant well" to hide the humiliation, pain, and betrayal of our abuse. As a result, we also deny the pain of others and fail to feel compassion or sympathy for other people who are suffering or in need: because we deny the victim in ourselves, we refuse to see it in others either (Gillette & Moore, 1991). For the most part, our shadows go largely unnoticed and remain repressed and outside our conscious awareness. However, specific people and situations from our past can suddenly trigger or activate a part of our shadow and render us unskillful in a tense moment (Hollis, 2008). I will discuss this obstacle next.

Emotional Obstacle 3: Shadow Activation—
When the Past Haunts the Present

Despite our best efforts to suppress and hold uncomfortable parts of our personalities outside of our awareness, our shadows are often triggered or activated by people and situations that we associate with a past grief or trauma. When this happens, we suddenly find ourselves on "high alert" despite there being no immediate threat to us. We become disproportionately defensive, angry, aggressive, guilty, or anxious without a rational reason for feeling such things (Hollis, 2008; Jung, 1969; Zweig & Wolf, 2009).

For example, some people become activated by a messy room or apartment because they were often chastised for being messy while growing up. They suddenly become anxious and feel like someone is "going to get it" if things are not cleaned up immediately. I have found that other people become triggered by tardiness, especially if they grew up with one parent who was always running late and another parent always criticizing the lateness. If they must wait 10 minutes for a late friend to join them for lunch, they erroneously begin to think, "This person just does not care about me or our friendship at all." The fear and anxiety associated with experiences of implicit bias are akin to the defensive fears of shadow activation; both are rooted in the unconscious and in the experiences of childhood.

As I've mentioned prior, recipients of discrimination and biased behaviors also face the added challenge of managing the emotional charge they may still be carrying from past traumas and humiliations. When past events or people trigger an emotional charge that recalls the original suppressed pain, it adds to the cognitive and emotional effort needed to deal with feelings in the present moment (Hollis, 2008). One defense mechanism we have against acknowledging such victimized moments (among other painful things we deny in ourselves) is to "see" such traits in others and then condemn them for possessing them.

Emotional Obstacle 4: Shadow Projection—
Accusing You of What I Deny in Myself

It can be challenging and even distressing to acknowledge one's shadow. In order to defend ourselves from acknowledging these suppressed parts of our personalities, we project our shadows onto those people that display the troubling traits we deny in ourselves (Johnson, 1993). Phoebe Cramer's series of studies show that that when a person's ego or self-esteem is threatened, they will project their own negative traits onto others (Cramer, 1998, 2003, 2006, 2007). Projection is defined as "attributing one's own unacceptable thoughts, feelings, or intentions to others, so as to avoid the anxiety associated with harboring them" (Cramer, 2006, p. 23). It is a kind of cognitive bias that results in the perception that the world is more negative and ominous than it truly is in objective reality (Cramer, 2007). Projection is both a cognitive mechanism and an intensely emotional experience (Conte & Plutchik, 1993). It occurs when people feel threatened and highly anxious, and it is characterized by a mixture of negative emotions, including hostility, disgust, and self-hatred (Plutchik, 1995). Projection functions as a normal defense mechanism in childhood but becomes a destructive and dysfunctional obstacle to adulthood. Given its capacity to act as a cognitive bias that generates high emotional arousal, it follows that projection often functions as an antecedent to destructive conflict (Mortenson, 2007, 2017).

In his seminal study of roommate conflict, Sillars (1981) demonstrates that particular conflict attributions, such as increased blame of the other person and the sense that conflicts are stable rather than situational, are dysfunctional and associated with lower relationship satisfaction. Conflict strategies are influenced by the attributions people make about the situation and the other person in the conflict. The difference between different attributions and their effects on conflicts cannot be underestimated (Canary, 2003). When people make benign attributions, they favor more cooperative conflict strategies with their partners that emphasize collaboration and information sharing (Sillars, 1981). They tend to express less defensiveness (Gottman, 1994) and demonstrate greater control over the impulse to act destructively (Berkowitz, 1993).

We explored the role of shadow projection in roommate conflict by first constructing a shadow projection questionnaire that focused on three trademark qualities that are present when someone projects onto another person (Mortenson, Creasy, & Geyer, 2020). First, the target person comes to represent a socially risky aspect of the projector's own past and activates the projector's defenses (Johnson, 1993). Second, the projector experiences an emotional paradox, simultaneously disapproving of and envying the target person (Zweig & Wolf, 2009). This envy represents a hidden desire on the part of the projector to get away with the same behaviors he/she condemns in the target person. Third, the projector actually feels as if he/she is being personally judged by the very person he/she vigorously criticizes. In other words, projectors accuse others of judging them for things they unconsciously critique in themselves (Mortenson, 2017). For example, I may be running late to meet a friend for lunch and think to myself, "I bet they're thinking I'm so flakey because I'm not on time." When I arrive, my friend is perfectly content to begin lunch when I arrive.

Using correlational analysis, we found that roommate projection predicted relational dissatisfaction, increased perceptions of negative roommate behaviors, increased negative attributions against the roommate, increased negative behaviors like frustration and anger against the roommate, and most importantly, increased destructive conflict strategies related to avoidance and aggression (Mortenson, Creasy, & Geyer, 2020).

We then placed projection into a structural equation model based on Sillar's proposed sequence of attribution, emotion, and behavior. Projection was placed as an antecedent to negative attribution alongside issue severity, relational satisfaction, and the roommate's perceived behaviors. Projection emerged as the strongest predictor of negative attributions against the roommate. Negative attributions, in turn, predicted negative emotions against the roommate as well as destructive conflict behaviors (Mortenson, Creasy, & Geyer, 2020). In summary, our exploratory study suggests that shadow projection contributes significantly to the kinds of negative attributions that drive destructive conflict.

I found similar patterns when I examined the influence of teammate projection on both positive and negative emotions, attitudes, and teammate behaviors with data collected and analyzed for this chapter. After my university's Internal Review Board certified that my research posed no risks to participants, ensured their anonymity, and provided for their informed consent, I was allowed to collect data. I surveyed 464 college undergraduates about their recent experiences on a team project and asked them to fill out a general projection scale and a team-specific projection scale. Participants also filled out scales by (Van Dyne & LePine, 2017) that measured both positive teamwork dynamics such as group identity, interpersonal justice, self-expression, influence on decisions, cooperation, trustworthiness, helping teammates, consulting others, encouraging others, peacemaking, equity in work, reciprocity, and general satisfaction as well as negative teamwork dynamics, including team dissatisfaction, fighting with teammates, letting others do all the work, and taking over the project from "lazy" teammates.

After ensuring that all instruments showed appropriate factor structure and levels of reliability, I ran a series of correlation analyses. Correlational analysis showed that general projection (the tendency to project one's own negative attributes onto people in general) was highly correlated with team-specific projection (the tendency to project one's negative attributes onto teammates) $r(462) = .473, p < .01$. This suggests that people with a strong sense of generalized projection are highly likely to project on specific people as well.

Further correlational analysis showed that both general projection and teammate projection are linked to increases in negative behaviors and attitudes toward teammates, as well as in decreases in positive teammate attitudes and behaviors. For example, general projection showed a range of small, but significant negative correlations for feeling respected by teammates $r(462) = -.177, p < .01$, overall team satisfaction $r(462) = -.160, p < .01$, cooperative discussion $r(462) = -.118, p < .05$, perceived equity in decisions $r(462) = -.102, p < .0$, fairness in work contribution $r(462) = -.132, < .01$ (see

Table 3.1. Descriptive Statistics and Correlations for Projection and Positive Teamwork Behaviors

Variable	n	M	SD	1	2	3	4	5	6	7	8
1. Gen proj	462	2.63	9.77	1							
2. Team proj	462	2.51	9.33	.473**	1						
3. Respected	462	2.61	.985	−.177**	−.202**	1					
4. Cooperate	462	2.57	.975	−.118*	−.182**	.691**	1				
5. Equity	462	2.83	1.25	−.102*	−.206**	.507**	.694**	1			
6. Fair share	462	2.76	1.11	−.132**	−.203**	.531**	.682**	.829**	1		
7. Reciprocat	462	2.57	1.02	−.122**	−.225**	.603**	.721**	.729**	.760**	1	
8. Satisfaction	462	2.55	1.29	−.160**	−.191**	.549**	.624**	.545**	.368**	.344**	1

** $p < .01$; * $p < .05$.

table 3.1). Generalized projection also demonstrated a number of small, but significant positive correlations for overall team dissatisfaction $r(462)=.207$, $p<.01$, fighting with teammates $r(462)=.116$, $p<.05$, letting others do all the work $r(462)=.120$, $p<.01$, and taking over the project from supposedly "lazy" teammates $r(462)=.170$, $p<.01$ (see table 3.2).

When the focus of projection is narrowed to teammates, the strength of the correlations increased. For example, teammate projection was negatively associated with feeling respected $r(462)=-.202$, $p<.01$, cooperative discussions $r(462)=-.182$, $p<.01$, perceived equity in decisions $r(462)=-.206$, $p<.0$, fairness in work contribution $r(462)=-.203,<.01$, and reciprocity in helping teammates $r(462)=-.225$, $p<.01$ (see table 3.1). Teammate projection also showed a number of positive correlations with dysfunctional team attitudes and behaviors such as team dissatisfaction $r(462)=.342$, $p<.01$, fighting with teammates $r(462)=.256$, $p<.01$, letting others do the work $r(462)=.198$, $p<.01$, and taking over the project from "lazy" teammates $r(462)=.160$, $p<.01$ (see table 3.2).

Given the significant correlations between teammate projection and negative team perceptions and behaviors, I ran a multiple linear regression with teammate projection predicting levels of team dissatisfaction, fighting with teammates, letting others do the work, and taking over for "lazy" teammates (see table 3.3). A significant regression equation was found for team dissatisfaction (F(1, 462) 60.8 $=p<.001$) with an $R^2.117$ $R^2_{Adjusted}=.115$). The analysis showed that teammate projection predicted levels of team dissatisfaction (B $=.404$, $t(462)=7.8$, $p<.001$, ^{power} 1.0). A significant regression equation was also found for fighting with teammates (F(1, 462) 32.37 $=p<.001$) with an $R^2.066$ $R^2_{Adjusted}=.067$). The analysis showed that teammate projection predicted how much participants fought with their teammates (B $=.274$, t(462)=5.96, p< .001, ^{power} 1.0). Letting others do the work also produced a significant regression equation (F(1, 462) 32.37 $=p<.001$) with $R^2.066$ $R^2_{Adjusted}=.064$). Teammate projection predicted how much participants let other teammates do the project work (B $=.21$, $t(462)=4.3, p<.001$, $^{power}.991$). A significant regression equation was found for taking over the project from "lazy" teammates (F(1, 462) 12.1 $=p<.001$) with an of $R^2.026$ $R^2_{Adjusted}=.024$). Teammate projection predicted how much participants took over their group projects for "lazy" teammates (B $=.219$, $t(462)=3.4$, p< .001, $^{power}.935$).

Taken together, these results suggest some important characteristics of shadow projection. (1) Like other emotional phenomena, projection operates as both a state and a trait. Cramer's studies do an excellent job of showing us that projection can be a state that is activated in people when they feel their self-esteem is threatened. In other words, well-adjusted individuals can be induced to project negative traits onto others. The exploratory studies I have presented suggest that projection is also an emotional trait and that some

Table 3.2. Descriptive Statistics and Correlations for Projection and Negative Team Work Behaviors

Variable	n	M	SD	1	2	3	4	5	6
1. Gen projection	462	2.63	9.77	1					
2. Team projection	462	2.51	9.33	.473**	1				
3. Fought teammates	462	5.80	1.23	.116*	.256**	1			
4. Free riding	462	5.82	1.22	.120**	.198**	.766**	1		
5. Took over project	462	5.09	1.58	.170*	.160**	.531**	.439**	1	
6. Dissatisfaction	462	5.20	1.36	.207**	.342**	.698**	.616**	.517**	1

** $p < .01$; * $p < .05$.

Table 3.3. Regression Analyses: Teammate Projection and Negative Team Behaviors

Variable	Estimate	SE	95% Confidence Interval		p
			Lower	Upper	
Dissatisfaction	.404	.242	3.020	3.983	.001
Fought Team	.274	.049	.175	.366	.001
Free Riding	.210	.051	.105	.304	.001
Took Control	.219	.062	.094	.340	.001

individuals are "high projectors" whose generalized state of projection is increased when focused on specific people like roommates and teammates. (2) Projection appears to have three distinct but related elements: the target person represents a socially risky aspect of the projector's own past. The projector simultaneously disapproves of and envies the target person. The projector feels judged by the very person he/she condemns. (3) Shadow projection contributes significantly to dysfunctional thoughts, feelings, and behaviors in interpersonal conflict; further, it works against healthy teamwork attitudes and behaviors and aggravates maladaptive teamwork behaviors. Now that we have a better understanding of the emotional obstacles that we ourselves bring to challenging situations and people, I will describe the Strengths and Shadows Deep Personality Assessment and present how it addresses these issues.

THE DEEP ASSESSMENT: RAISING EMOTIONAL AWARENESS AND INCREASING INTERPERSONAL SKILLS

There are many personality assessments currently being used in business and education. Popular among them are the Myers-Briggs, The Big Five Personality Test, Enneagram, Strengths Quest, DISC, and True Colors (Myers & McCaulley, 1988; Goldberg, 1990; Riso & Hudson, 2000; Tupes & Christal, 1992). The Strengths and Shadows Deep Assessment differs from these tests in two major ways: first, the assessment focuses on the interpersonal and social aspects of the personality rather than on the intrapersonal and solitary sides of the self. Second, the assessment identifies and integrates our conscious personal strengths with their unconscious shadow sides. Third, the Strengths and Shadows assessment presents learners with an emotional "disorienting dilemma" that becomes part of a transformative experience geared toward their personal growth and change.

A Strategic and Interpersonal Approach to Personality

Personality assessments and tests often strive for either a comprehensive or a strategic focus for mapping and describing the personality. For example, the Strengths Quest and True Colors tests tend to focus on positive sides of personality (Crews, Bodenhammer, & Weaver, 2020). In contrast, the Myers-Briggs attempts to identify and distinguish among 16 basic personality preferences (in their healthy and dysfunctional states) to provide a basic, but comprehensive portrayal of personality (Myers & McCaulley, 1988). Similarly, one of the most popular personality assessments, The Big Five, describes five major personality traits in terms of their weaker and more extreme senses. I argue here that these assessments present a largely reductionist and static view of the personality and fail to capture the ways that people change (emotionally and behaviorally) across different situations and relationships (Goldberg, 1990).

Based on relational psychology and communication science, the Strengths and Shadows assessment presents a strategic and interpersonal model of personality. This model of personality focuses on the different emotional, interpersonal, and communicative challenges that people attempt to manage in order to be effective in leadership roles, with colleagues at work, and more deeply connected to family and friends. As such, the Strengths and Shadows assessment emphasizes the social aspects of personality over the solitary and internal. While some assessments focus on more internal challenges like emotional reactivity, open-mindedness, introversion, and organization, Strengths and Shadows emphasizes emotion-based communication challenges such as holding boundaries, speaking one's truth, dealing with criticism, relinquishing control, and forms of personal influence.

When participants do the assessment, they are first asked to imagine themselves involved in a specific context with a particular person or group of people in their life (i.e., speaking out at a team meeting, discussing finances with a spouse, helping a child with homework, and deciding chores among roommates). Situating the assessment interpersonally helps participants see that different parts of their personalities are activated and engaged by different people and situations. Moreover, the assessment helps them to discern which of their personal strengths and shadows are activated by specific people and activities in their lives.

Assessing the Unconscious Side of the Personality

A deep personality assessment provides a balanced understanding of a person's strengths and challenges, and it identifies the connections among those factors. In this way, we can learn to recognize our own dysfunctional and destructive tendencies so we can embody the best message strategies in the moment of a challenging situation. Many personality assessments like The Big Five, Myers-Briggs, True Colors, and Strengths Quest have made use of Carl Jung's concept of the four psychological functions, that is, thinking, feeling, intuition, and sensation, as well as the psychological focus of introversion versus extroversion (Myers & McCaulley, 1988; Tupes & Christal, 1992). However, these tests all fail to integrate other vital concepts from Jungian thought into their assessments: most notably, the psychological shadow and shadow projection. The Strengths and Shadows assessment helps learners identify both their conscious personal strengths and the psychological shadows that they bring to different situations and relationships.

After identifying a specific person and situation, learners choose the top 4 or 5 most relevant personal strengths that they bring to the situation out of a total of 12 strengths. Learners choose their top strengths from a list or from a deck of specially developed cards. I have also developed and used a personality test in which learners distinguish their top traits from the answers they give on the test. After learners have chosen their top strengths, the shadows that accompany those specific strengths are revealed to them and they are given time to read about these shadows and the effects they have on other people. In this way, learners confront the dysfunctional side of their strengths and identify specific sources of emotional difficulty for themselves. For example, learners who choose Order as a top strength (i.e., the ability to structure situations, manage people, and direct projects) find that Order is attached to Anxious Controlling (i.e., micro-managing people, lacking flexibility, taking over projects, and failing to trust others). Moreover, they realize falling from Order into Anxious Controlling is a simple matter of being triggered by some unconscious fear from the past that has invaded their present moment. After they have been given sufficient time to internalize the shadow material, learners are then presented with some initial strategies for managing their specific shadows (which are expanded upon later in the intervention).

The moment when we confront our own shadows is crucial; it is a reckoning with the self that brings about humility, recognition, and the beginning of transformation. Unless we are forced to confront our dysfunctional and reactive sides, we will not be equipped to confront the dysfunctions in our relationships or larger society. We will, once again, fall into the emotional disconnect between knowing the best things to say and do, but not actually saying or doing them.

In this book, we approach issues like implicit bias as an interpersonal problem that is increasingly solved between people (Czopp & Ashburn-Nardo, 2012). We may have to skillfully hold others accountable for their biased behavior just as others may hold us accountable for ours. In either case, managing and communicating about biases and biased behaviors is difficult and can easily lead to feelings of anger and defensiveness (Bosson, Pinel, & Vandello, 2010). As such, confronting the dysfunction and ethical problems of our own (and others') implicit bias and privilege calls for a kind of courage, humility, and emotional mastery that requires what transformative learning scholars call a "disorienting dilemma."

A Vital and Disorienting Dilemma

To be a transformative experience, a deep assessment requires a confrontation with the self and a disorienting dilemma that pushes learners to critically reflect on who they are and how they act. Transformative learning theory suggests that when learners have their beliefs and/or identity challenged in the learning environment, they experience a disorienting dilemma which may initiate other changes in their meaning structures (Mezirow, 1994; Mezirow & Taylor, 2009). The disorienting dilemma may be associated with a particular life crisis or function as a progressive sequence of insights leading to changes in perspectives and behaviors (Mezirow, 1994; Mezirow & Taylor, 2009). As a result of transformative learning, students often experience strong feelings and emotional upheavals as their values and beliefs undergo a paradigm shift (Cranton, 1994). However, anger, grief, and frustration are usually replaced by excitement and confidence as learners gain a new sense of empowerment (Grabov, 1997).

By critically reflecting on their behaviors and experiences, learners begin to understand how and why the assumptions they have about themselves constrain the way they perceive, feel, and respond to different people and situations. As learners gain awareness of the sources of their assumptions and the consequences of holding them, their habitual patterns of perception and expectation become more inclusive and more discriminating. If learners actually begin to make choices, or otherwise act upon their new understandings, they have been changed by what they have learned (Mezirow, 1997).

Transformative learning focuses on both reason and emotion to create an environment that helps students connect reason and logic with feeling and intuition (Taylor, 1998). Reason-based activities involve critical thinking, self-reflection, and writing. Learners also share and reflect on their experiences and assumptions through class discussions (Mezirow, 1991). Emotion-based activities employ a learner's own feelings and emotions as a means of personal reflection and emotional discernment through the use of effective sources such as symbols, images, and archetypes (Cranton, 1994). As a process, discernment involves three stages: receptivity, recognition, and grieving. First, an individual must be receptive or open to receiving "alternative expressions of meaning" and then recognize that the message is authentic (Boyd & Myers, 1988, p. 277). Grieving takes place when learners realize that old patterns or ways of perceiving are no longer relevant. This realization moves them to establish new ways of perceiving that they can integrate into their worldview.

The Strengths and Shadows assessment follows a similar pattern of receptivity, recognition, and grieving. Asking learners to first choose their personal strengths relative to a person and situation puts them into a receptive state of mind. These are, after all, positive traits that they consciously favor. When it is revealed that these personal strengths are also linked to reactive and dysfunctional sides of their personality, learners go through a process of recognition and grief. They are forced to acknowledge and reckon with these "inferior" sides of themselves. This concept of personality allows learners to see that their personal strengths are also connected to some of their most acute challenges. This first confrontation not only helps learners to acknowledge and accept that they have dysfunctional and challenging aspects of themselves; it also helps them see that the same personal strengths that help them succeed can turn dysfunctional when they are emotionally set off or activated by threatening stimuli. As the supportive confrontation intervention continues, learners face further difficult sides of their behavior as they learn about the triggers that activate their shadows and the kinds of shadow projections they put upon different people in their life.

Ultimately, the goal of transformative education is to assist learners in questioning their assumptions, considering multiple points of view, and acting upon what they have learned (Cranton, 1994; Mezirow, 1991; Taylor, 1998). As learners gain awareness of the sources of their assumptions and the consequences of holding them, their habitual patterns of perception and expectation become more inclusive and more discriminating.

Research suggests that transformational education empowers students and enhances their self-confidence, provides greater resources for taking action and gaining control over their lives, and provides insight into their connections with others (Courtenay, Merriam, & Reeves, 1998; Taylor, 1998). For example, transformative education proves effective for teaching life skills to families on public assistance. Participants cited activities that required them to critically assess their perspectives on nutrition, parenting, and allocating resources as key to adopting a more self-sufficient lifestyle (Christopher et al., 2001). Further, a number of researchers report on the success of transformative approaches to diversity education (Boyd, 2008; Curry-Stevens, 2007; Dass-Brailsford, 2007; Doucet & Adair, 2013; Kerssen-Griep & Eifler, 2008; Middleton, Anderson, & Banning, 2009; van Gorder, 2007).

The Goal: Supportive Confrontation

The Strengths and Shadows assessment is the first part of a four-part intervention geared toward helping people learn and embody forms of supportive confrontation. Supportive confrontation occurs at three levels. First, learners confront and identify their shadows and the dysfunctional emotions that come with them. Second, learners identify the things that trigger their shadows and learn to manage these emotional upheavals. Third, people confront their emotions interpersonally in order to discern and defuse the kinds of interpersonal defense mechanisms that may render them unskillful with others. Finally, people integrate and employ message strategies designed to foster supportive confrontation. Forms of supportive confrontation allow us not only to support an individual while critiquing their behavior but also to help us better permit others to confront their own difficult and upsetting circumstances.

As you saw at the beginning of the chapter, before Janice skillfully offered supportive confrontation strategies to help Kyle better understand his racist and sexist comments, she confronted her own shadows around her experiences with discrimination as well as her shadows around confrontation. She also worked to defuse any predator shadows around Kyle. When she began speaking to him, she moved quickly to defuse his defenses by contrasting how he might take her advice (being labeled a bigot) by what she really meant by it (bringing more awareness to his good intentions). Janice also spoke to what was mutually important to both herself and Kyle—the emotional well-being of a valued colleague. She also discussed that she harbored biases and that doing so was a human thing. Finally, she invited him to participate in an initial solution (raising his awareness by watching a video about implicit bias).

In summation, supportive confrontation involves more than saying "the right things" when confronting another person; it means putting oneself into the correct emotional frame before and during a confrontation and, further, being mindful of both the emotional and instrumental goals of a confrontation. When these emotionally supportive components are embodied in our approach to a confrontation, the sophisticated and skilled communication messages needed to deescalate and resolve a confrontation come more naturally and have a greater effect on the situation and people involved (Mortenson, 2017).

Chapter 4

What Happens When We Are Mindful in Communication?

Xiaowei Shi

Since this chapter is about mindful communication, let's think about a time that calls for mindfulness in communication: the pandemic in 2020.

As it may be the case with many of you, the year 2020 left a heavy mark on our memories. To me, it was a time for contemplating human resilience. I remember almost every day, I needed to watch TV to get the COVID-19 updates. I also needed to take time to go outside, stand under a thick hackberry tree in my backyard, look at clouds and sometimes gaze at the stars, simply to clear my mind.

In this year, we witnessed the worst pandemic in a century, with a contagious novel corona virus (COVID-19) spreading across the world with thousands of people dying every day. Sadness, loss of normalcy, anxiety, and despair were just a few salient terms to describe our feelings during this year. It deeply touched me when I saw people from all walks of life, including frontline medical professionals, grocery workers, teachers, neighbors, and many more, choose courage, dignity, and compassion over fear to respond to this deadly disease.

On the other hand, however, I also observed a seemingly impasse in human communication. This is related to my observation that there seems to be no common ground for people to communicate with each other. For example, some people choose not to wear their face masks or maintain social distance for a variety of reasons, despite the scientists' pronouncement that simply following these rules can save lives. Through social media, as well as talking with neighbors and friends, I realized that we actually consume drastically different news sources to form our perceptions of the world; some watch nothing but *Fox News*, whereas others get their news reports from the *New York Times*.

I understand that people prefer seeking information from news sources they consider reliable (e.g., conservative versus liberal and mainstream versus social media). But when people resist or ignore other alternatives, then we are in a situation where we compare apples and oranges when talking about reality. Of course, I'm sure there are many individuals who refuse to depend on only one source for information seeking. They would like to examine the same news from both liberal and conservative sides as well as news reports from foreign agencies (e.g., BBC World News). As a result, we receive different versions of reality.

Our different beliefs and information-seeking preferences not only divide reality into different versions, but they can also sever close-knit family relationships. Sharp disagreement on issues can happen between mother and daughter, husband and wife, and coworkers and close friends. People choose not to talk to one another due to bitter, hurtful arguments.

To add even more tension to our nervous system, 2020, was also a presidential election year. Many of us, including my colleagues, close friends, and I, joined the public and private dialogues and debates on many issues centered on which candidate best represents American values and will lead the nation in the direction we felt was right. We get angry, sad, or disappointed when the other party disagrees with what we believe as the fundamental issues, such as justice, fairness, or freedom. I asked myself, "If disagreements are inevitable, then what would be the core values that will sustain us rather than divide us?" I also wondered: "How can we manage the cacophony of divergent views in today's society? And what is the likelihood of creating a mutual understanding if we perceive different realities?"

On second thought, I noticed that all the questions I have raised are based on the assumption that good reasoning will solve all our problems. Wait a second. What if human communication is not built solely on rationalities? What if it is our unconscious biases, implicit preferences, or routine communication habits, rather than different lines of reasoning, that create all the communication barriers? That is, barriers in mutual understanding may derive from our own personal cognitive "noises," which prevent us from seeing what the others see.

This utterly new angle of thinking generates a new set of inquiries. For example, if rational reasoning isn't the only ingredient of problem-solving in a human communication context, then what are the other ingredients?

This is why *mindfulness* in communication becomes relevant for this inquiry. Mindfulness is a communicative choice, in which communicators seek different sources in the context and are willing to manage seemingly contradictory voices in order to make a well-adapted response to the current situation. As this definition reveals, mindful communicators adapt to the current communication situation when they offer a certain line of reasoning. They pay attention to the interaction process, in which a series of argumentative episodes unfold over time (e.g., arguments, counterarguments, and emotional reactions). Furthermore, mindful communicators take note of the "seemingly contradictory voices" and seek to identify the "real" underlying concerns, hence moving the problem-solving process forward.

You may say, "That is easy. If I spend a little more time in examining what comes to my mind and thinking about what I want to say or respond, I could do a whole lot better in communication." As you will see in the following chapter, mindfulness entails more than "paying more attention" or "thinking hard." Cognitive effort only helps in certain areas of communication—but not in all. With all these questions in mind, let's start our exploration in this chapter.

MINDFUL COMMUNICATION

According to Burgoon and Langer (2012), the state of being mindful entails active information processing in face of a specific situation, during which individuals pay attention to the novel cues in the current context and elaborate on one's own resources in order to respond to the situation. As a result of staying alert to the changes in the current context, individuals in a mindful state are more likely to question whether a canned, or "ready-to-use," manner of responding to the situation is effective or not. If yes, then go ahead. This process is very fast, almost automatic. If no, however, then individuals will decide to modify their behavior, or they may choose to maintain a particular behavior based on their deliberate thinking.

In contrast, a mindless state involves inactive processing (Burgoon & Langer, 2012). According to Burgoon and Langer, mindlessness does not mean no reasoning or no thinking at all. Rather, it is often associated with certainty of cognitive assessment, and certainty somehow reduces the need to question whether one's responses to a situation are effective or not. For example, inactive processing can occur when individuals feel certain that they are in a familiar situation, experiencing recurrent events, or conducting routinized behavior.

Cognitive Elaboration

Mindful behavior requires cognitive elaboration. The term "cognitive elaboration" focuses on the elaboration of cognitive thinking, which involves active situational and procedural evaluations. For example, imagine that you receive a job offer, but the starting salary is significantly lower than what you expected. But this job is important for you, so you need to think very carefully about what to say before negotiating with your employer about increasing your starting salary. That "thinking" is cognitive elaboration, which involves recognizing situational constraints and deliberating upon different ways to respond to a certain social interaction (Burgoon & Langer, 2012; Langer, 1989).

Mindless behavior, on the other hand, triggers limited cognitive elaboration that is induced by situational familiarity, low motivation, stress and fatigue, or other forms of distractions. Can you think of a few situations when you are more likely to be in a mindless behavior mode? For example, I would say it is mindless when I wash dishes while listening to music, when I greet a friend in a hallway, saying "Good morning," or when I know exactly what I want to say and just want to say it out quickly. In these situations, I may use little cognitive effort. As the following section on automaticity illustrates, we need automatic thinking and relatively mindless behavior to save energy and to function well in daily life. Many mindless behaviors are a result of familiarity and prolonged practices. They provide a foundation for us to function in daily life.

Depending on how motivated and capable individuals are in assessing a person, an issue, or a position, people selectively invest their effort to engage in issue-relevant thinking (Petty & Cacioppo, 1986). Moskowitz et al. (1999) explained this kind of cognitive flexibility in the following way. On the one hand, people can rely on prior knowledge, heuristics, stereotypes, scripts, and schemas to deal with life and events. This process is rather quick and effortless as people already have a mental architecture of the contents and sequences of an action. On the other hand, people can expend time and effort to analyze a situation, identifying, differentiating, and integrating relevant information so as to form a well-adapted response.

Interestingly enough, rather than rational thinking, heuristic-automatic processing is actually our *default* thinking mode (Gigerenzer, 2000; Klaczynski, 2001). Heuristics are "simple decision rules or rules of thumb that typically lead to reasonable decisions with minimum effort" (Wilson, 1995, p. 17) or a "simplified model of the world" (Gigerenzer, 2000, p. 259). People have the capacity to do both systematic and automatic processing (Moskowitz et al., 1999). While one thinking mode dominates, the other may continue to affect the behavioral outcomes in ways that may not be consciously controlled (Chen & Chaiken, 1999; Petty & Cacioppo, 1986). So, it is rare that individuals can totally suppress one process over the other.

Automaticity in Communication

Is automaticity in communication analogous to mindless behavior? The answer is not exactly. Automaticity in communication can involve both mindless and mindful communication. For example, if an automated communication is goal-oriented and strategic, then it results in a mindful behavior (Bargh & Chartrand, 1999; Kehneman, 2012).

Here is a real-life example. There are many situations when my students asked brilliant questions that I could not address effectively on site. What would I do? I have an automatic but sensitive way to respond. I would say,

> This is an excellent question! Very thoughtful. As I have not fully examined that part of the literature yet, let me check first, gather more knowledge, and I will get back with you in our next class. In the meanwhile, you keep searching for your answers. We will discuss together in class.

This response is prepared, hence being uttered in a relatively automatic way. But I am also mindful. As you have seen, I make sure to address two issues at hand—an appreciation of the question and my intention to fully examine the literature before giving a response. In this way, both of our communication needs (or desirable social images) are addressed.

Let's explore the two facets of automaticity in communication. On the one side, automatic behavior provides a foundation for us to function in daily communication. Many times, automatic execution due to prolonged practices helps generate effective and possibly accurate decision-making in communicative interactions. For example, we can sense a person's frustration simply by noticing the changes in speed or tone of one's talking. Bargh and associates' research (1999, 2001, 2006) elucidates this automaticity aspect in communication. According to Bargh and Chartrand (1999), frequent and consistent pairing of situational features with goals, ones that people chronically selected in those situations, can result in automatic behavior.

Therefore, the first facet of automaticity is efficiency. Many times, automatic thinking or planning process may bypass the conscious attention step. Based on experimental studies, Bargh and Chartrand noted that such automaticity between goals and behaviors applies to both relatively complex self-regulatory goals and simpler behavioral goals. To put it differently, many of our automatic communication behaviors are developed overtime through practices in multiple contexts. They work well for us.

The second facet of automaticity is on the flip side of efficiency—the sacrifice of quality. Sometimes, automatic behavior generates less-than-optimal communication. It provides efficiency at the cost of ignoring the distinctions between the current situation and past experience. Indeed, research findings reveal that, rather than being neutral (or fair) in judgment, our automatic, habitual ways of thinking can result in unintended bias, such as maintaining or reinforcing certain judgments and actions over others (Greenwald & Banaji, 2017; Petty & Cacioppo, 1986).

Understanding this side of automaticity helps us address the question: "How can we manage the cacophony of divergent views in today's society?" To manage disagreements, we may need to re-examine our own automatic thinking and strategically confront the other's automaticity. Due to our prolonged exposure to certain beliefs, values, narratives, and different cultural and social-economic backgrounds, every one of us has developed a working mental framework to view things in a certain way and to express our opinions. To gain a sense of perspective from another person's point of view, we may first need to recognize and then sometimes to *resist*, automaticity in our own communication. Furthermore, we need to pay attention to the other party's implicit intentions, unexpressed needs, even biased thinking because the other party is also likely to be in her or his own automatic model. That is, mindful behavior involves a two-way monitoring work—our own communication and our partner's communication behavior.

AN ILLUSTRATIVE EXAMPLE

If we take our familiar path to construct a message, we would be likely to get into our automatic thinking mode. To overcome automatic reactions to a certain situation, we may have to pick up situational cues very carefully. Here is one illustrative example based on my own teaching experience:

> One day, after our first Public Speaking class, Jimmy came to me and wanted to talk. He was calm and polite ("Jimmy" is a pseudonym). Jimmy told me that he is highly anxious about giving a speech in front of an audience. He is introverted and very shy. He asked me how to survive this course.

I know I cannot use the strategies that work for other students, saying something as, "The more you practice, the more you will feel better." Such advice is not helpful because it implicitly endorses a mindset of "practice makes perfect." As you may have noticed, in the current context, there is an important clue that Jimmy revealed to me—he is very shy. This clue trigged me to think, "What about giving speeches to a virtual audience?"
This is what I said to Jimmy:

> Thank you for talking with me, Jimmy! Introverted individuals are very creative and have a lot of thoughtful ideas. My own 10-year-old daughter is an introvert, and through her, I get the chance to see the "beautiful mind" of an introverted person. I think you will have a lot to contribute to our class. Now the concern is about how to feel more comfortable in preparing and delivering speeches.
> First of all, our course will start with several mini-speeches. They are not graded. You will gradually build your confidence in these tiny steps. On the

other hand, I wanted to let you know that there is an option for you get the same course credit by taking an online class. Many students do not know, but our department offers an online public speaking course. If you like, I can help you switch to that online course.

That online course allows students to submit their pre-recorded speeches by posting a video link on the discussion board. If you don't want to stand before a live audience, this online course may be an option. Your professor and classmates will watch your video-taped presentations and provide feedback. So, you have two options, either staying in this class or switching to an online format. What do you think?

In the preceding message, in addition to signaling care and support, I engaged self-disclosure about my daughter. I also provided new information about the "pre-recorded" speech option in an online course. Does this response count as mindful communication according to our definition in the previous section (e.g., well-adapted, offering a novel solution)? What do you think?

The reality was like this. After hearing this message, I remember Jimmy smiled. He liked what I said. Jimmy chose to stay in the class, and he received an "A" in that course.

To continue our discussion on mindful communication, in what follows, chapter 5 will present a research project. It is a two-study investigation of how organizational members attempt to persuade their supervisors on work improvement. This research seeks to address two questions: (1) Does mindful communication bring in qualitatively better messages? and (2) Does mindful communication result in bias-free messages, treating a male versus a female leader in an equal manner?

Chapter 5

Empirical Research on Mindful Communication

Xiaowei Shi

MINDFULNESS AND IMPLICIT BIAS IN UPWARD INFLUENCE: A TWO-STUDY INVESTIGATION

When we disagree on how things should work in our organizational life, we may attempt to influence each other. One type of such influence is upward influence. It is defined as a "deliberate attempt by a subordinate to select tactics that will bring about change in a more powerful target and facilitate achievement of a personal or organizational objective" (Waldron, 1999, p. 253). Upward influence is purposeful and strategic (Shi & Wilson, 2017), but such subordinate-supervisor exchanges do not always occur in a smooth and bias-free manner. As the following literature review will illustrate, one factor that potentially generates *noises* in upward communication is our implicit attitudes (IAs) on gender-role expectations toward our male versus female leaders.

Gender-related implicit bias refers to people's underlying preferences or hidden beliefs about gender roles in the workplace (Mortenson, 2017). Researchers found that, in evaluating men and women with identical job qualifications, people show a tendency to prefer *men* over women in leadership positions (see Isaac et al.'s "systematic review," 2009; Koenig et al.'s "meta-analysis," 2011). Such subtle, sometimes unintended, acts of discrimination create career challenges and emotional stress for female leaders (Johnson et al., 2008; Mortenson, 2017).

Against this backdrop, the present research investigates whether organizational members use different approaches to communicate with male versus female managers when facing an identical work situation. There are two main reasons that justify the worthiness of the present research. First, it offers evidence regarding whether there are differential communicative practices privileging male over female leaders on a daily basis. Such evidence is theoretically important because it helps explain how mundane communication tasks can sustain and fuel-biased action along gender lines. Critical approaches to organizational studies suggest that organizational members' identity and power relations are instantiated and maintained "in the routine discursive practices of everyday organizational life" (Mumby & Stohl, 1991). Daily language choice (also called "strategy-as-practice") shapes and structures organizational being (Cooren et al., 2011; Putnam & Cooren, 2004). By bridging IA literature and upward influence research, the current research complements the efforts in this line of inquiry.

Second, this research extends current literature on gender-related IAs by examining employees' underlying perceptions and preferences on a leader's gender role. Through comparative tests, it clarifies whether employees assess their relationships with male versus female leaders differently in terms of perceived relational closeness, power distance, and level of comfort in addressing a male or a female manager. Such findings will shed new light on the cognitive underpinnings that give rise to gendered upward influence communication behavior.

As an additional contribution, findings of such investigation hold relevance to organizational training on gender equity. Recent research reveals that implicit gender-role bias can be corrected when people realize that certain unconscious bias interferes with their fair judgment (Girod et al., 2016; Isaac et al., 2009). The evidence gathered from the present research may offer new insights on how implicit gender attitude manifests in subtle ways in our daily communication.

IMPLICIT ATTITUDE AND COMMUNICATION

According to Greenwald and Banaji (2017), IA refers to a mental process whereby our underlying preferences or hidden beliefs, bypassing conscious awareness, exert influence on our judgment and current action. Take gender-based IAs as an example. Such attitudes are formed during our early social experience, but they remain powerful in affecting judgment even after we have received formal education to change those attitudes (Greenwald & Banaji, 2017). As Hill (2016) reported, even for people who explicitly support and value gender equality, they sometimes "find that their implicit biases work against their intentions" (p. 1).

To tap into people's unconscious attitudes toward leadership roles, researchers commonly employ the Implicit Association Test or "IAT" (Greenwald & Banaji, 2017). IAT assesses how quickly people can associate gender categories (e.g., "he" versus "she"; or a male versus female name, "Kevin" versus "Karen") with different evaluative concepts, such as a "leader" versus a "follower." One consistent finding in IAT research is that organizational members could not associate leadership roles equally with men and women.

Regardless of one's own gender or feminist beliefs, participants show a slight-to-moderate implicit gender bias in favor of associating males with leadership roles (Implicit Association score $d < .30$; Greenwald & Banaji, 2017). Data from AAUW's study on gender gap ($n > 4,000$) confirmed the existence of such kind of bias (Hill, 2016). According to AAUW report, "Even people who identify as feminists still have a slight tendency to associate men with leadership" (Hill, 2016, p. 2).

In addition to IAT research findings, other empirical evidence in multiple disciplines also demonstrates that gender bias exists in organizational life. In a study on political voting decisions, Mo (2015) found that implicit bias favoring men in political leadership roles exerts a significant direct influence on people's actual vote choice. Isaac et al. (2009) conducted a systematic review of 27 experimental studies on how organizations evaluate job candidates. They found that regardless of the raters' own sex, people tend to evaluate male applicants more positively than female candidates who have identical qualifications. Similarly, a meta-analysis by Koenig et al. (2011) confirmed that contemporary organizational members still associate leaders with a male image prototype (intra-class correlation = .62).

From a social interaction perspective, communication researchers emphasize that ongoing communicative interactions can reconstruct attitude formation in organizational life. Such a position is articulated by Mumby and Stohl (1991). According to them, communicative interactions serve as a "primary vehicle through which social relations are produced and reproduced" (p. 315). That is, organizational process is a perpetual state of becoming (Fairhurst, 2007, 2009). Gender difference is initiated and sustained in the workplace through practicing differences (West & Fenstermaker, 1995).

This line of literature highlights the constitutive role of communication. It is likely that the symbolic meanings (e.g., respect, approval) that messages carry through daily communication toward a male versus a female leader contribute to the gender difference. Yet, no substantial work to date has explored in detail how subtle message choices, such as being more or less polite, may inadvertently contribute to this biased communication process. This becomes the central focus of the present study.

DISTINCT FEATURES OF UPWARD INFLUENCE

This study focuses on upward influence behavior because of its innate face-threatening feature. It involves an attempt to persuade a person of higher positional power to do something otherwise he or she would not do, such as suggesting to change a work procedure. It is consequential yet risky. If it is done skillfully, upward influence fulfills multiple functions in one's career development, including demonstration of work dedication, impression management, and relationship building (Buzzanell, 2000; Waldron, 1999). Such a behavior, however, is inherently face-threatening to both parties. For example, if a subordinate tells a supervisor how to improve a current work operation, he or she runs the risk of threatening the supervisor's face as a competent leader. Moreover, the subordinate should recognize the threat to his or her own face; he or she may appear "nosy" or "know it all."

Because of this face-threatening feature in communication, upward influence communication requires employees to manage face threats in their message choices (Brown & Levinson, 1987). This unique feature provides a platform for the present study to examine if employees address face concerns equally or differently depending on whether they talk to a male versus female supervisor.

In particular, employees' upward influence message features are examined along the dimensions of reasoning, expressed approval, and implied pressure (see Shi & Wilson, 2010; Falbe & Yukl, 1992). To mitigate face threats, employees can use reasoning to frame a message to make certain courses of action appear more reasonable and beneficial than others (Botero & Van Dyne, 2009; Shi & Wilson, 2010). Presumably, such utterances have implications for both parties' positive face needs as task oriented. Past research also noted that subordinates use approval expressions and low-pressure tactics to show respect and deference toward a superior (Falbe & Yukl, 1992).

If gender-related biased communication exists in upward influence, then we would observe differential reliance on rationality and politeness to show deference when employees communicate with a male versus a female leader about an identical work problem. Although organizational members are aware of the face concerns in upward influence, this study speculates that they may not necessarily honor a male and a female supervisor's face needs in the same way. Consistent with prior literature on gender-related bias in favor of male leaders, this study speculates that employees vary their effort to address face threats in upward influence in favor of a male manager. Two hypotheses are raised:

> *H1.* On average, employees' upward influence messages will exhibit a greater level of reasoning when communicating with a male than with a female supervisor.

H2. On average, employees' upward influence messages will include more approval expressions (H2a) and exert less pressure (H2b) when communicating with a male than with a female supervisor.

MINDFULNESS

As an initial inquiry, this study seeks to clarify whether mindfulness can reduce the impact of gender-related implicit bias in workplace communication. Mindfulness increases people's attention to draw distinctions between current context and routinized strategies employed in the past (Langer, 1989). Mindless communication, on the other hand, is characterized as limited information processing when people enact communication by drawing upon routinized strategies. Burgoon, Berger, and Waldron (2000) observed that some spouses fall into habitual ways of expressing disgruntlement to their partners and, in response, their partners tend to use the same withdrawal strategy (e.g., stonewalling) regardless of contexts.

As IAT research reveals that human minds possess automatic associations between gender categories (i.e., male versus female) with social roles (i.e., leader versus follower), it is likely that gender-related IA is a heuristic cue. Researchers noted that when individuals are in a less mindful state of mind, a few familiar cues (e.g., affect heuristic of "gut feeling, or abstract concepts, such as "men are leaders") are sufficient to trigger judgments (Skagerlund et al, 2020; Walkins, 2015). That is, people will stop processing the rest of the available information and rely on those heuristic cues to enact behaviors. If IA is a heuristic cue, then the differential politeness toward male versus female leaders may only show a low mindfulness condition. Such differences will disappear when employees are in a high mindfulness pattern of thinking.

On the other hand, however, IAs may *persist* under a mindful mindset. According to Petty and Cacioppo (1986), biased processing may occur as part of high cognitive elaboration. In such kind of high elaboration mindset, people prefer to think in particular ways, such as "favoring the maintenance or strengthening of the original schema" (Petty & Cacioppo, 1986, p. 19).

Although mindfulness prompts people to pay more attention to situational cues, it may not equally or uniformly contribute to communication qualities toward a male versus a female supervisor. An increase in attention to the current situation may inadvertently strengthen the bias toward male over female leaders.

This part of the discussion suggests that mindfulness can either remove gender-related bias (if it is a heuristic cue) or enhance such a bias (if it is indeed a cognitive preference). To fully explore how mindfulness plays a role in upward influence communication, a research question is raised:

RQ1. What is the impact of mindfulness on upward influence communication?

STUDY I

Data for Study I were collected as part of a larger project at multiple organizations in the western and midwestern United States during 2008–2009 after having received IRB approval.

Participants

A total of 212 full-time employees (116 male, 96 female) were recruited through an online research participation system at the researcher's university. This system allows students to participate in research if they have full-time work experience or if they help recruit qualified participants in exchange for extra course credit. According to participants' own descriptions of their most recent jobs, 63% of them worked in sales and service-based positions; 23% worked as technicians, accountants, and other professional positions (e.g., software-engineer, financial analysts); and roughly 12% worked in government offices, army, schools, and hospitals. The majority of the participants were between 20 and 30 years old (81%). Their average work experience in a full-time position was 4.57 years. Most participants are Caucasians (n=155, 73%), whereas 12% of participants identified themselves Asian Americans, 7% Hispanic American, 1% African American, and 6% identified as other, including Middle Eastern, Indonesian, South Asian, and multiracial.

Procedure

Participants completed an anonymous online survey on Qualtrics website (Qualtrics, Provo, UT). A total of eight conditions, crossing mindfulness (low versus high), supervisor gender (female versus male), and upward influence scenario (workplace testing result problem versus training problem) were randomly distributed when a participant started the survey. The randomization is operated by Qualtrics.

At the beginning of the survey, they were reminded of the voluntary nature and the purpose of the study, which stated, "This questionnaire asks you to imagine what you would say or do in a situation in which you were trying to influence your supervisor at work."

Next, participants read a scenario, in which they imagine they are an employee who has noticed a work-related problem and wanted to propose a desirable solution to the work problem. The scenario has two versions (testing result problem versus training problem). Each participant randomly received one version. The scenario describes in detail what the work problem is about and what the employee wants to propose to his or her supervisor.

All participants received same information except that half of the participants were told that they were about to talk to "Bob," who was referred as "him"; whereas the other half were about to talk to "Barb," who was referred as "her."

After reading the scenario, participants were asked to write down their messages as if they were sitting in the manager's office and started to "talk" to either Bob or Barb.

Following this upward influence message construction section, participants completed measures of realism check, self-assessment of mindfulness, a demographic questionnaire, and other measures that did not particularly pertain to the current research questions.

Manipulation

Mindful Communication

To induce mindful thinking, this study incorporated three manipulation techniques that are commonly used in the research on cognitive elaboration, including task importance (Petty, Harkins, & Williams, 1980), personal relevance (Johnson & Eagly, 1989), and a reminder of thinking about the current situation carefully.

In this segment of the survey, participants in the high mindfulness condition received information about "your opinions will weigh heavily in this final research design" (high task importance). In contrast, participants in the low mindfulness condition were told that "your responses will be combined into a large data set" (low task importance). Participants in the high mindfulness condition also received information about "your company has an incentive policy for contributing good suggestions" (high personal relevance) and a reminder to think carefully by considering all the relevant information in the context. Participants in the low mindfulness condition, however, did not receive these two pieces of information.

Instrumentation

Realism Assessment

Participants completed a two-item measure of perceptions of realism for the scenarios: "The scenario is believable" and "The scenario is realistic" ($\alpha = .89$). The t-test comparing realism scores of the two scenarios revealed no significant difference (training problem: $M = 5.47$, $n = 105$; testing problem: $M = 5.54$, $n = 107$, $t(210) = -.453$, $p = .65$).

Mindfulness Self-Assessment

Participants completed a two-item measure of mindful communication (adapted from Dillard, Segrin, & Harden, 1989), including "I put a lot of thought into figuring out what is the best way to persuade Barb (or Bob)" and "I put a great deal of effort into persuading Barb (or Bob)" (1 = *strongly disagree*, 7 = *strongly agree*), α = .84. The two items were averaged to create an index of mindfulness ($M = 5.02$, $SD = 1.23$).

Message Coding

The reasoning dimension of upward influence is coded by counting the amount of reasons that are presented in a message. A reason is defined as a distinct statement made by a subordinate in explanation or justification of why a request or suggestion is being made (Wilson & Kunkel, 2000). The coding procedure involved identifying each distinct (nonrepetitive) phrase that justifies why one's suggestion is needed, desirable, feasible, and so on. As such, a key task in this coding procedure is to unitize reasons in each message. Guetzkow's U index of disagreement is used to check coding reliability $[U = (O_1 - O_2)/(O_1 + O_2)]$, where O_1 presents the number of reasons identified by coder 1 and O_2 represents the number of reasons identified by coder 2. Folger, Hewes, and Poole (1984) describe U's < .10 as indicating a low degree of disagreement about unitizing.

In addition to the author (identified as coder 2), a graduate student (identified as coder 1) was hired to code message reasoning, who was unaware of this study's design. After a training session, the two coders coded data independently. Guetzkow's index was checked at two intervals. Both U's were less than .05. After resolving disagreements, each participant's reason units were summed to create a score for the amount of reasoning.

The politeness of upward influence is coded along the dimensions of expressed approval and pressure. Two other graduate students were hired for this part of the coding (coder 3 and coder 4). Each message was rated, in its entirety, for the overall level of approval and pressure on 1–5 scales. The coding manual was adapted from Cai and Wilson (2000). *Approval* dimension assesses a subordinate's effort to make the supervisor feel positive or supported rather than negative or threatened (1 = strong disapproval, 5 = strong approval). *Pressure* refers to how much room a subordinate leaves a supervisor in complying, ranging from making a supervisor feel she or he must do what is recommended (5 = high pressure) to making a supervisor feel like he or she has a choice about whether to comply (1 = low pressure).

Cohen's Kappa (Folger, Hewes, & Poole, 1984) was calculated to check agreement. The equation for calculating Kappa is Kappa $= (P_o - P_c)/(1 - P_c)$. Here P_o indicates the observed percentage agreement among coders and P_c is the proportion of agreement that would have agreed by chance. Kappa values of .50–.75 represent moderate-to-high levels of intercoder agreement (Hale & Fleiss, 1993). In the training session, 20 messages from the data were selected. A 5 × 5 contingency table was set up with two coders, five categories (1 = low, 5 = high). Kappa was .94 for the overall intercoder agreement for expressed approval and .90 for implied pressure. Disagreements were resolved through discussion. The training ended when both coders agreed on the coding procedure and criteria. Next, the two coders categorized all messages independently. Cohen's Kappa was .94 for approval and .92 for expressed pressure. The final data were based on the coding results after disagreements were resolved.

Results

Descriptive data are reported in table 5.1. Each upward influence message has an average of 5.94 reasons. Upward influence messages produced by participants were close to the mid-point in both approval ($M = 2.88$, $SD = .70$) and pressure ($M = 2.75$, $SD = .83$).

Manipulation Check

Participants in the high mindfulness condition reported a considerably greater effort in thinking about what to say than those in the low mindfulness condition ($M = 5.47$ versus 4.62), $F(1, 204) = 28.15$, $p = .001$, $\eta^2 = .12$, $d = .73$. No three-way interaction effect was found. These results indicated that an intended high versus low mindfulness condition was successfully set up.

Table 5.1. Descriptive Statistics in Study I ($N = 212$)

	1	2	3	4
1 Mindfulness	1	.50**	−.01	.07
2 Reasoning Quantity		1	−.01	.14*
3 Approval			1	−.51**
4 Pressure				1
M	5.02	5.94	2.88	2.75
(SD)	(1.23)	(3.31)	(.70)	(.83)
High Mindfulness ($n = 100$)				
M	5.47	6.80	3.01	2.65
(SD)	(1.05)	(3.51)	(.74)	(.85)
Low Mindfulness ($n = 112$)				
M	4.62	5.16	2.77	2.86
(SD)	(1.24)	(2.94)	(.63)	(.79)

*$p < .05$; **$p < .01$; ***$p < .001$.

The supervisor's gender had a significant main effect ($M=5.20$ versus 4.85), $F(1, 204)=4.12$, $p=.05$, $\eta^2=.02$, $d=.30$, indicating that participants who read a male supervisor scenario, compared to those who read a female supervisor scenario, reported a higher degree of mindfulness in message construction.

The two upward influence scenarios (workplace testing method versus training) did not yield any main or interaction effects on mindfulness and gender, neither on message features nor perceived realism in the upward influence situation, suggesting that two scenarios do not differ in significant ways that will affect data analysis. As such, they were collapsed in analysis.

Gender Effect on Reasoning

ANOVA analyses were conducted crossing mindfulness and supervisor gender for message reasoning feature. Mindfulness exerted a significant main effect on amount of reasons offered by participants to their hypothetical supervisor, $M=6.80$ versus 5.16, $F(1, 208)=13.25$, $d=.51$. Messages produced by participants assigned to the high mindfulness condition generated more reasons when providing upward feedback to their supervisor as compared to those participants assigned to the low mindfulness condition. This result suggests that mindfulness improves message reasoning level.

Results revealed no significant difference in how many reasons were offered by participants assigned to the male versus female supervisor conditions, $M=6.12$ versus 5.77, $d=.10$, There was no mindfulness × gender interaction effect, $F(1, 208)=.002$, $p=.97$, $\eta^2=.00$.

Thus, *H1* regarding whether there is a supervisor gender effect on message reasoning feature was not supported.

Gender Effect on Politeness

ANOVA analyses were also conducted crossing supervisor gender and mindfulness for message approval and pressure features. Results revealed that mindfulness had a main effect on message politeness features. Messages produced in high mindfulness condition exhibited a significantly higher level of approval ($M=3.01$ versus 2.77, $d=.34$) and a lower level of implied pressure than those in the low mindful condition ($M=2.62$ versus 2.86, $d=-.30$). This result indicates mindfulness increases message politeness.

The overall level of approval ($M=2.94$ versus 2.85, $d=.10$) was similar across the male and female supervisor conditions. However, interaction analyses revealed that participants assigned in a high mindfulness thinking condition expressed a significantly higher degree of approval to a male supervisor in comparison to a female supervisor ($M=3.22$ versus 2.78;, t (98)=3.05, $d=.62$). In the low mindfulness condition, however, there was no such difference toward a male versus a female supervisor (see table 5.2).

Such a pattern provides partial support for H2a. That is, organizational members expressed a higher approval level in favor of a male supervisor when they think carefully about what to say. In a low mindfulness thinking mode, however, there is no gender effect (see figure 5.1).

The supervisor's gender exerted a main effect on a message's pressure dimension. The degree of implied pressure expressed toward a female supervisor was significantly higher than that toward a male supervisor ($M=$ female: 2.87 versus male: 2.63), F (1, 208)=4.06, $p=.05$, $\eta^2=.02$. $d=.30$. H2b was supported.

Interaction analyses further revealed that employees assigned in a high mindfulness condition expressed a lower level of pressure to a male supervisor in comparison to a female supervisor ($M=$ male: 2.38 versus female: 2.86), t (98)=-2.76, $d=-.56$. In the low mindfulness condition, however, there was no such difference toward a male versus a female supervisor (see figure 5.2).

These patterns in the high mindfulness condition are consistent with the bias effect of supervisor's gender. Employees tend to enhance their politeness styles in favor of a male leader under a mindful thinking mode. As such, the results suggest that mindfulness in communication did not correct gender bias effect. Rather, it reinforced the impact of gender effect on message features. *RQ1* is addressed.

Table 5.2. Summary of ANOVA Analysis Assessing Gender Effect on Reasoning and Politeness in Study I

Source	df	F	η^2
Reasoning			
Mindfulness (A)	1	13.25***	.06
Supervisor gender (B)	1	.45	.00
A × B	1	.002	.00
Approval			
Mindfulness (A)	1	5.17*	.02
Supervisor gender (B)	1	.98	.00
A × B	1	13.85***	.06
Pressure			
Mindfulness (A)	1	5.26*	.02
Supervisor gender (B)	1	4.06*	.02
A × B		4.26*	.02
Error	208		

*$p<.05$; **$p<.01$; ***$p<.001$.

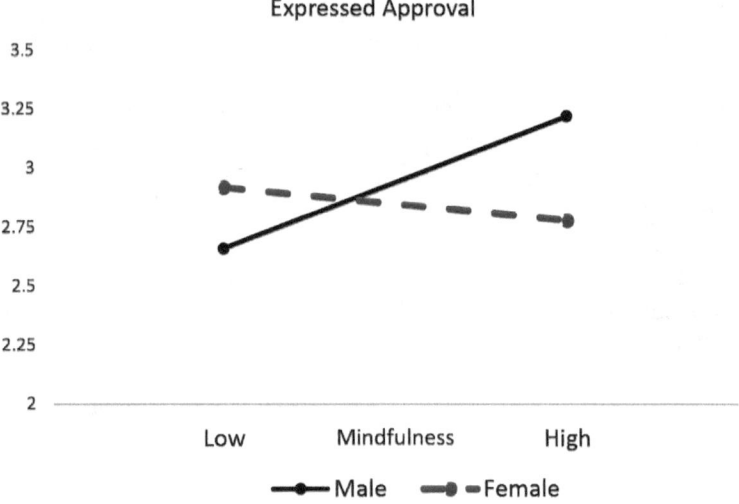

Figure 5.1. Interaction Analysis of Mindfulness and Supervisor's Gender on Approval in Study I.

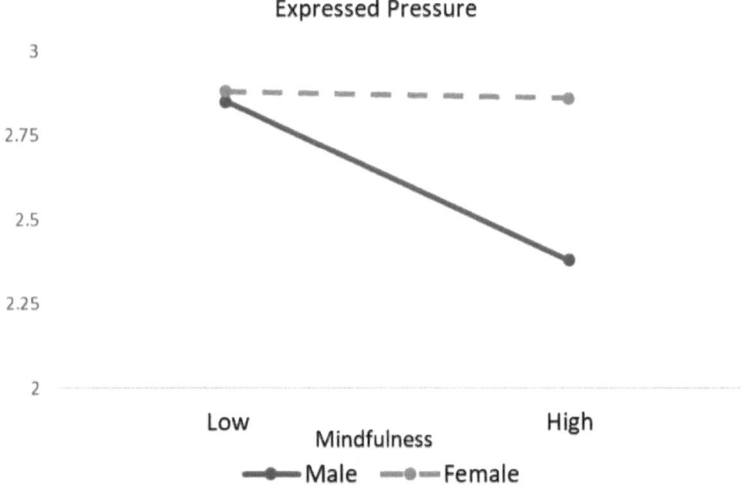

Figure 5.2. Interaction Analysis of Mindfulness and Supervisor's Gender on Pressure in Study I.

Discussion of Study I

Situated in an upward influence context, Study I examined whether employees chose different politeness strategies when talking to a male versus a female supervisor. Some interesting results surfaced from Study I. First, as expected, mindfulness does increase communication quality in the sense that message reasoning and politeness features are improved. Participants in the high mindfulness condition produced messages with higher levels of reasoning and politeness in comparison to those in the low mindfulness condition.

Second, data revealed that participants used a similar level of rational reasoning to both male and female leaders, but they used less polite strategies to communicate with a female leader than with a male leader by expressing a higher degree of pressure level during upward influence ($d=.30$).

Third and finally, increased mindfulness seems to bring about biased communication, rather than correcting it. Biased communication is defined as unfair treatment in language use based on gender roles that are irrelevant to the judgment of a person's worth or competence (Dovidio & Gaertner, 1986). In particular, data revealed that a heightened degree of mindfulness did not correct employees' differential behavior toward male versus female leaders. Participants in the high mindfulness condition expressed a higher degree of approval ($d=.62$) and a reduced pressure level to a male supervisor ($d=-.56$) but not to a female supervisor.

These findings are consistent with implicit bias literature. That is, people tend to show a slight-to-moderate implicit gender bias in favor of male leadership roles regardless of one's own gender or feminist beliefs (Greenwald & Banaji, 2017). In the present study, the leader's gender effect on message politeness is also in the range of small-to-medium effect sizes ($d=.30\sim.62$).

In summary, using a similar method that is commonly employed in the IA research, Study I provided initial evidence that subtle influence of gender-related implicit bias has an impact on message choices.

There is one question, however, worth further examination. From a communication perspective, it is the situational assessments that give rise to different communication strategies that people select to use (Dillard et al., 1989; Samp & Solomon, 1998; Wilson, 2002). In the current study, an unexplored but important question is: What situational and relational factors underlying gender-related IA may account for employees' differential communication? Study II was conducted to address this question.

STUDY II

Data for Study II were collected in a large comprehensive university in the southeast region of United States in 2019 after having received IRB approval.[1]

Study II replicates the procedures in Study I. In addition to the influence message construction section in the questionnaire, Study II added situational and relational assessment measures toward male versus female leaders. By definition, attitude consists of cognitive and emotional facets of a person's evaluative knowledge toward an object (Greenwald & Banaji, 2017; Fazio, 2007). Such evaluative knowledge can be feelings or perceptions of an object (Insko & Schopler, 1967).

To tap into people's attitudes toward male versus female leaders, the present research proposes to examine perceived power distance and relational distance. Politeness theory (Brown & Levinson, 1987) suggests that increased perceived power and relational distance would lead people to choose more polite strategies in communication. Self-categorization theorists Hogg and Terry (2000) suggested that, as being more prototypical, male leaders have more status-based power than female leaders who are less prototypical.

In an upward influence context, this means that male leaders may have presumed power over followers by virtue of fitting a prototypical image in comparison to female leaders. As such, the following two hypotheses are raised:

H3. In an upward influence context, subordinates perceive greater power distance when communicating with a male manager than with a female manager.

H4. In an upward influence context, subordinates perceive greater relationship distance when communicating with a male manager than with a female manager.

While perceived relational and power distance are related to cognitive facets of attitudinal assessment, "feeling comfortable" is an important emotion-based attitude (Petty et al., 2003). As such, this research includes employees' comfort in talking with a supervisor as the third attitudinal factor. It is hypothesized that female leaders are more likely to instantiate certain feminine qualities during interaction, hence being seen by the subordinate as being friendly and nonthreatening. A hypothesis is stated:

H5. In an upward influence context, subordinates feel greater levels of comfort when communicating with a female manager than with a male manager.

Participants

Participants were recruited through an online research participation system managed by the author's institution. This system allows college students to participate in research or help recruit qualified participants in exchange for extra course credit. A total of 154 participants completed the online experiment (80 women, 74 men, $M_{age}=20.29$, age range: 18–48). About 60% of participants reported that they had more than 2 years of work experience; 27% had 1–2 years of work experience; and 13% had at least 1 year of work experience on a full-time position. About 59.7% of participants identified themselves as Caucasian, 17.5% as African American, 8.4% as Hispanic, and 7.1% as Asian American.

Procedure

In this online experiment, a total of four conditions, crossing upward influence contexts (talking to a manager versus college professor) and the superior's gender (female versus male) were randomly distributed to participants. At the beginning of the survey, they were reminded of the purpose of the study, "The purpose of this study is to gain insight about how feelings and thoughts about one's work supervisor or college professor may affect how we talk to him or her."

Next, participants read a scenario randomly assigned by Qualtrics Online Survey. In the business manager scenario, the content is about updating an old testing method (same as in Study I), in which half of the participants were told that they were about to talk to "Bob," whereas the other half were about to talk to "Barb." In the college professor scenario, the content is about a student who makes suggestions to a professor on a group project assignment. Half of the participants were told that they were about to talk to "Dr. Kate Smith," whereas the other half were about to talk to "Dr. Karl Smith."

After reading one version of the scenarios, participants were asked to write down their actual messages. The procedure was intended to prompt participants to respond to the following situational assessments and message quality assessments that were provided in the next section of the questionnaire. In the end, participants filled in a demographic questionnaire and other measures that do not particularly pertain to the current research questions.

Instrumentation

Situational Assessment

Participants were asked to think back to the scenario and indicate their perceptions of power distance and relational distance while imagining talking to a male versus a female manager (or a professor). A perceived power distance item is stated as follows: "In terms of relative power distance between Bob/Dr. Karl Smith and me, I feel he has ____ me" (1 = "Much less power than" to 5 = "Much more power than"). A relationship distance item is stated: "In general, while I am meeting with Barb/Dr. Kate Smith, I feel my relationship with her is __" (1 = "Very close" to 5 = "Very distant").

Participants were also asked to think back to the scenario and indicate how comfortable they feel talking to a male versus a female manager (or professor) by considering all the relevant aspects of the situation. It is stated, "In general, while I was meeting with Barb, I felt." The scale was anchored from 1 = "Not comfortable at all" to 5 = "Very comfortable."

The decision of using single-item scale was made based on the following rationale. Single-item scale allows participants to weigh all those aspects that they view as relevant and provide an overall rating on an attitudinal object (Nagy, 2002). Research on single-item measurement reported that it is reliable if the measurement meets two major criteria: (1) the construct is narrow in scope and unambiguous to the respondents and (2) the measurement item is stated sufficiently clear and concrete (see de Boer et al., 2004; Gardner et al., 1998; Wanous et al., 1997). Study II used clearly stated single-item measurement to serve this purpose.

Message Quality

Rather than coding written messages, Study II sought to directly measure the extent to which participants wanted to use reasoning and politeness to communicate with a superior during upward influence. As such, participants were told to think again about the message they just wrote and evaluate their own message features. Message reasoning, disapproval, and demand (or pressure) are adapted from Lim and Bowers (1991) on a five-point scale (1 = *strongly disagree*, 5 = *strongly agree*). The reasoning scale has two items: "to explore possibilities for her (him) to consider" and "to suggest ways to make our work even better" ($\alpha = .87$).

A single item on disapproval expression was used, "to express my disapproval of the current situation" (1 = *strongly disagree*, 5 = *strongly agree*). Finally, a single item was employed to gauge how much a participant wants to use pressure to persuade a superior, "to demand what I want forcefully" (1 = *strongly disagree*, 5 = *strongly agree*).

Results

Zero-order correlations, means, and standard deviations for the measures are presented in table 5.3. The data was normally distributed with skewness and kurtosis scores ranging between −1 and +1. ANOVA and follow-up pairwise comparison analyses revealed three similar findings that were observed in Study I.

First, consistent with Study I, across two contexts, the overall level of reasoning in upward influence messages did not differ by gender conditions, $F(1, 150) = 1.52$, $p = .35$, $\eta^2 = .01$. *H1* was not supported.

Second, an interaction effect crossing context and gender on expressions of disapproval was significant, $F(1, 150) = 3.95$, $p = .05$, $\eta^2 = .03$. To decompose this interaction effect, an individual *t*-test was conducted separating

Table 5.3. Descriptive Statistics of Study II ($N = 154$)

	1	2	3	4	5	6
1 Relational Distance	1	−.30**	−.02	−.09	−.09	.05
2 Comfortableness		1	.09	.05	.03	.19*
3 Power Distance			1	.00	−.01	.16
4 Demand				1	.23**	.01
5 Disapproval					1	−.07
6 Reasoning						1
M	2.81	3.09	4.15	1.88	3.02	3.75
(SD)	(.78)	(.93)	(.72)	(.90)	(1.05)	(.89)

*$p<.05$; **$p<.01$, ***$p<.001$.

the workplace context and college professor context. While the disapproval expressed by students to professors did not differ by gender in the academic condition ($M=3.39$ versus 3.32), $t(75)=.31, p=.76$; gender effect is observed in the organizational context. Consistent with Study I, participants expressed a higher level of disapproval toward a female supervisor in comparison to a male supervisor ($M=2.95$ versus 2.38), $t(74)=2.58, p=.012, d=.60$. Hence, H2a was partially supported. This pattern is depicted in figure 5.3.

Third, participants reported they expressed more demands (or pressure) toward a female superior than they did toward a male superior in both the academic and organizational contexts, $M=$ female: 2.01 versus male: 1.73, $F(1, 150)=3.96, p=.04, \eta^2=.03, d=.32$. Hence H2b was supported. This pattern is depicted in figure 5.4.

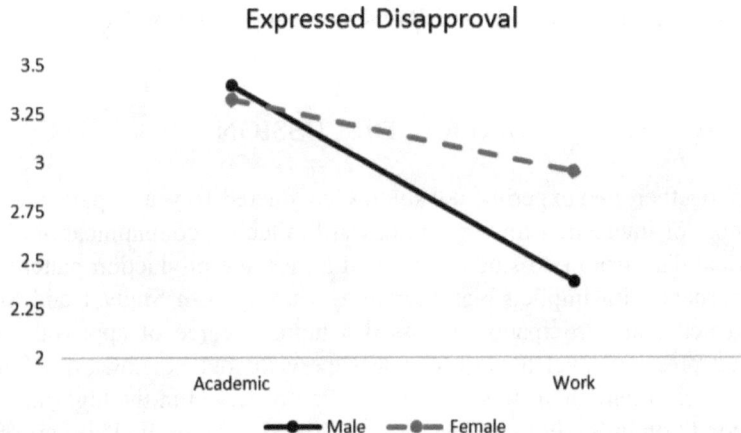

Figure 5.3. Interaction Analysis of Context and Superior's Gender on Disapproval in Study II.

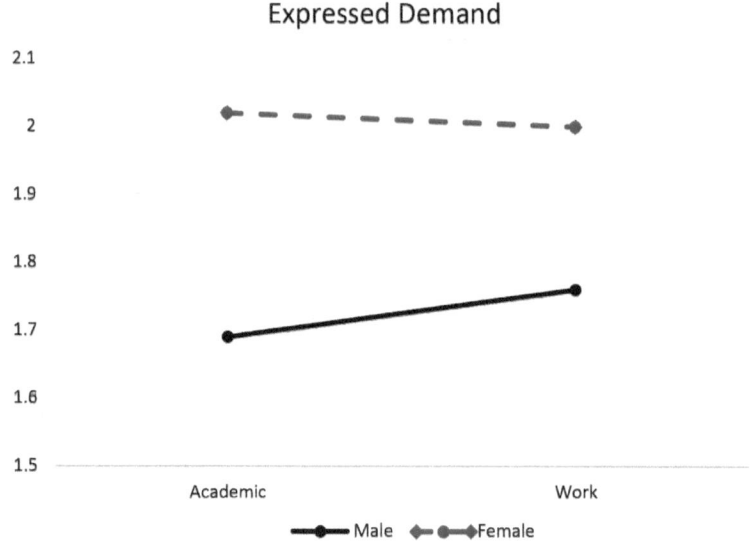

Figure 5.4. Interaction Analysis of Context and Superior's Gender on Demand in Study II.

Fourth and finally, to determine whether relational distance, emotional comfort, or power distance are perceived differently under the influence of employees' gender-related attitude, ANOVA was conducted. Results revealed that participants reported a higher level of comfort in communicating with their female superiors than male superiors ($M = 3.25$ versus 2.92, $F (1, 150) = 4.95$, $p = .03$, $\eta^2 = .03$, $d = .36$). H5 was supported.

Perceived relational distance and power distance, however, did not vary across conditions, hence, H3 and H4 were not supported (see table 5.4).

GENERAL DISCUSSION

Taken together, two experimental studies, conducted 10 years apart, revealed a number of interesting findings on upward influence communication. First, empirical data from two studies revealed a message production pattern that is congruent with implicit bias literature. That is, both Study I and Study II revealed that participants expressed a higher degree of approval and a reduced pressure level toward a male supervisor but not toward a female supervisor. In particular, this pattern was first observed in the high mindfulness condition in Study I and then was replicated in Study II. This part of the findings elucidates the existence of gender-related implicit bias in organizational communication.

Table 5.4. Analysis of Variance for Message Features and Situational Assessment of Study II ($N=154$)

Source	df	F	η^2
Message Features			
Disapproval			
Superior Gender (A)	1	2.36	.02
Context (B)	1	**18.44***	.11
A × B	1	3.95*	.03
Demand			
Superior Gender (A)	1	3.96*	.03
Context (B)	1	.02	.00
A × B	1	.09	.00
Reasoning			
Superior Gender (A)	1	1.52	.01
Context (B)	1	**36.02***	.19
A × B	1	.13	.00
Situational Assessment			
Comfortableness			
Superior Gender (A)	1	**4.95****	.03
Context (B)	1	.00	.00
A × B	1	.12	.00
Relational Distance			
Superior Gender (A)	1	1.70	.01
Context (B)	1	.62	.00
A × B	1	1.02	.01
Power Distance			
Superior Gender (A)	1	.00	.00
Context (B)	1	3.40	.02
A × B	1		
Error	150		

*$p<.05$; **$p<.01$; ***$p<.001$.

Second, interesting results also surfaced related to the comfort aspect in addressing female leaders. Study II revealed that participants see their male and female supervisors equally in terms of power distance and relational distance. But they reported a higher level of comfort in addressing their female leaders in comparison to male leaders.

In what follows, let's reflect upon some major findings of this research by relating to this chapter's main focus on mindful communication.

WHAT HAPPENS IN MINDFUL COMMUNICATION?

To address the question, "What happens if we communicate more mindfully?" the upward influence research reported here provides some insights. First, it finds that mindful processing results in qualitatively different messages. Mindfulness seems to lead research participants to produce advice messages with more detailed reasoning and more politeness features.

This finding provides new empirical evidence regarding the positive relationship between mindful processing and improved message qualities discussed by prior literature (Burgoon et al., 2000).

This finding is also consistent with Dr. Shi's dissertation study (Shi, 2009) examining communication goals and cognitive planning. In the dissertation, she reported some initial evidence (albeit suggestive) that, when research participants are less motivated to engage in mindful communication, they rely only on a few salient goals or thoughts in generating messages. In contrast, when research participants are in a high elaboration state of mind, they activate an array of thoughts and goals. Moreover, Dr. Shi found that people in a mindful state don't just have more thoughts in general; rather, they have more "cautious" thoughts that anticipate potential obstacles to or negative consequences from attempting to influence others. These thoughts lead participants to produce influence messages with more detailed reasoning and more politeness features.

BEING MINDFUL ABOUT WHAT?

The present findings also revealed that mindfulness does not decrease biased communication in the workplace. Indeed, Study I observed that a supervisor's gender effect occurs primarily when employees reported that they were thinking carefully about what to say. Participants in the high mindfulness condition who imagined talking to a male supervisor exhibited a higher degree of politeness (e.g., expressed approval and a reduced pressure level) than those who imagined responding to a female supervisor. In contrast, the gender-role-related effect did not exert any significant influence on the low mindfulness condition. So, contrary to the common knowledge that mindfulness will promote issue-relevant thinking (Burgoon et al., 2000; Langer, 1989), Study I discovered that increased mindfulness somehow reinforces people's gender-role-specific communication in favor of male leaders.

THE SUBTLETY OF BIASED COMMUNICATION

Taken together, results from two studies provide nuanced analyses of how daily workplace interactions reflect and fuel the seemingly divided communicative practices toward leaders through gender lines. On the surface, it seems that there is no gender-related bias in communication if we just focus on the reasoning aspect of upward influence messages. Participants in both

Study I and Study II used an equal amount of reasons in talking to their male and female leaders. However, this research revealed that the differential communication exists primarily in message politeness features.

For example, Study I found that employees expressed a significantly higher degree of implied pressure toward a female supervisor than a male supervisor. By examining in a different context, Study II revealed that college students expressed a higher degree of demand (or pressure) in talking with a female professor than a male professor on changing a class assignment.

Politeness carries symbolic meanings (e.g., respect, approval) in communication. This part of the research finding provides new insights about mindfulness communication. That is, subtle practices of biased communication in one form or another persist even in our mindful communication.

MINDFUL COMMUNICATION MONITORING: OUR INTERNAL AND EXTERNAL "NOISES"

What to Be Mindful About

Upon reflections on the research design and findings, let's start to think about the underlying motives of being mindful in communication. "What to be mindful about" seems to matter. For example, there is a distinction between being mindful of message qualities and being mindful of one's own "blind spot" in communication. In the present study, however, it seems that simply encouraging people to think carefully on how to communicate with others cannot reduce cognitive "noises" derived from gender-role stereotypes.

Hypothetically, it may help if an external reminder explicitly states, "Please think of the best way to persuade your work supervisor. Do not let irrelevant aspects (e.g., gender stereotypes) influence your message design." The effectiveness of this "explicit-reminder" technique calls for future research.

Managing Our Own Hidden Preferences

This chapter focused on upward influence to illustrate how implicit biases affect our daily communication. We are likely to witness and experience other forms of biased communication in other interpersonal communication contexts. A critical question arises: Can we come up with new ways of communicating with others by taking into consideration our own implicit biases?

To counter our automatic thinking with hidden-preference tendencies, some action-oriented strategies may serve the purpose. For example, simply telling oneself that "I need to be aware of my implicit biases" is overly vague. A higher level of mindful communication may require specific communication goals during a message planning stage. A communicator can set specific goals like "I want to try new ways to talk with her/him" or "If I want to develop a new *norm* in this relationship, I need to pay attention to my message choices in every single encounter with him/her from now on."

Tactful Response to Other's Biases

Mortenson (2017) suggested a range of strategies to respond to a biased behavior. The first strategy is to confront the biased message while not attacking the person. By focusing on how implicit bias is developed "as the social product or cognitive error" (p. 53), the speaker shows understanding of how easily people may fall into certain kind of unintended bias.

The second strategy involves addressing the face needs of the other party. For example, appreciating one's sincerity, asking more probing questions, or sharing stories of one's own experience. Mortenson (2017) emphasized that the purpose of such strategic communication is to create awareness and encourage cooperation. These strategies remind us the key role of mindful communication is to focus on the problem or task, not the person or emotion.

Take all together, the *message* is: Mindful communication doesn't just have more thoughts or more actions in general; rather, it has more cautious thoughts and takes more tactful actions.

NOTE

1. The author wishes to thank Dr. Tom Brinthaupt in the Department of Psychology at Middle Tennessee State University for giving feedback on questionnaire design and helping with data collection in Study II.

Chapter 6

When You Can Never See the World in the Way I Do

Xiaowei Shi

A few years ago, I received a faculty research-and-creative-activity grant from my institution in which I conducted interviews with 59 heterosexual couples (age range: 18–53). Among these couples, 20 couples participated in an interviews study only;[1] 39 couples participated in a laboratory observation study in addition to a face-to-face interview.[2] I called this project "What if you can redo a conflict." During the interviews, I asked participants to recall a conflict situation, one in which they had said something that ended up hurting the relationship very badly. I also asked, "Tell me about what you were thinking and feeling when you were in the conflict." Additionally, I asked, "If you could turn back the clock, how would you redo this conflict interaction differently? What would you do differently to make the experience more positive?"

During the laboratory study, each couple was videotaped while they sought to "redo" the conflict in order to get a more satisfying outcome. As I'm writing this chapter, I started to watch those videos and listen to their audiotaped conversations over and over again. The same awestruck feeling came back to me just like the initial time I talked with them during the interviews. Couples mentioned moments of disappointments and sadness (e.g., "She/he is always like this") as well as the sheer bliss of realizing that they still deeply love each other despite all their arguments (e.g., "You never told me that").

This project invited research participants to reflect upon their own conflict management behavior. During this process, participants had a chance to gain perspectives of the other's original intents and message choices. In addition, this project challenged participants to "reconstruct" their life stories by using a different communication method to engage in conflict resolution after their initial "unsuccessful" conflict talk.

Before introducing methodology and findings, let's start with a brief glimpse of how participants perceive conflicts in relationships. At the beginning of the interview, I asked an icebreaker question: "To what extent do you think you are an expert at handling conflicts in relationships?" Here are some highlights of their responses:

> I think I'm an expert because I've been in several conflicts with different types of relationships and with different types of personalities. The relationship I am in now, he doesn't respond to my argument. I will sit there and address my conflict with him. He just kind of sits there and looks at me because he doesn't deal with conflict. It's hard, but I like the fact that he is still listening. (Excerpt from a 20-year-old female participant)
>
> I wouldn't exactly say I'm an expert. I'm only 18. But to a certain extent, I know how to handle it. For example, if we get into an argument, instead of getting mad, just be calm, sit down, and try to talk it out. There is a difference between what you feel and what's actually happening. When you get the emotion involved into the situation, you can just blow up and hit the wall. But another way would be, you just sit back for a few seconds, then go, "Why did you do this?" You can understand instead of blowing up. (Excerpt from an 18-year-old male participant)
>
> I don't think, in any way, I'm an expert. But I think I learn things every time we have a conflict: how I deal with it, how it works, how it affects her. It helps me handle it next time. Hopefully, I'm continually getting better with conflicts. One specific thing is that I'm learning not to let my emotions dictate my response. If I'm frustrated or upset, (I'm) taking a few minutes before I respond to whatever we are dealing with. It helps me a lot with that emotional awareness, I guess. It's much nicer being aware of these things and how they affect other people, especially someone as close as my wife. It's nice to know that I'm getting better at that. (Excerpt from a 43-year-old male participant)

At a glance, do you see any common themes of how participants respond to their conflict experience across these illustrative excerpts? It seems that emotional reactions (e.g., having outbursts, remaining stoic, choosing calm) are part of the experience when couples deal with conflicts. It also seems that how individuals interact with each other through verbal and nonverbal message exchanges is essential to the conflict management process. Otherwise, it could become a fruitless, solo endeavor when the other party does not participate in the problem-solving process—for example, if that party shows stonewalling behavior.

Funnily enough, many couples told me that the interview time served as their "therapy session" because they felt they resolved their conflict through this interview experience. They indicated that they finally had the chance to clarify their original intentions, recognize their own limitations (e.g., "I didn't realize I was . . ."), and be able to see their conflict from other's point of view. Their comments reveal a hopeful aspect of conflict management. That is, it is possible to resolve a conflict if certain steps or procedures are taken during the conflict interaction process. Even if the initial conflict outcome was not satisfactory, couples still have a chance to "redo" it for a better result. With this observation in mind, this chapter explores the dynamic process of conflict interaction. One central question it seeks to address is: What procedural steps or communicative actions seem necessary for the conflict parties to gain perspectives from each other, such as "Okay, I think you're right" or "Yes, that's about it"?

METHOD AND PURPOSE

The Argumentative Interaction Management (AIM) framework (see chapter 2) proposes that individuals' implicit attitudes and lack of perspective-taking efforts help explain why communicators sometimes produce less-than-optimal, even hurtful, messages. This chapter focuses on perspective-taking efforts through the lens of examining conflict experiences of romantic couples.

After I obtained my institution's IRB approval for data collection, I started to post recruitment flyers on campus, describing the aim and procedure of this study and indicating that there is a small amount of monetary compensation for participating in this research. Couples can choose to participate in an interview-only study or a laboratory-and-interview study. Some participants were college students ($n=54$, about 45%), while others were students' parents or friends who heard about the research through word-of-mouth recommendations from students ($n=64$, about 55%). A total of 59 couples were recruited, of which 24 couples were married or engaged and 35 couples were in dating relationships.

All of the 59 couples participated in the interview sessions. Each interview lasted about 25–30 minutes, which took place at my office. Participants were informed of the voluntary nature of the study. I explained that they were free to leave the interview anytime they chose to do so and that there would be no penalty if they did not complete the whole interview. That is, they still would receive the same amount of monetary compensation even if they chose to exit the interview.

With participants' permission, all interviews were audio-recorded. Each interview followed a dynamic, nonlinear process, using open-ended questions. It consisted of three sections: (1) recalling a conflict situation; (2) gaining perspectives from each party's point of view: descriptions of what they said to each other during the conflict, what they were thinking during the event, and what they were feeling about the conflict situation; and (3) reconstructing the conflict: if they could turn back the clock, how would they redo this conflict? What would they do differently?

After the interview session, 39 couples chose to participate in a laboratory observation, which occurred in a psychology lab in the same building where my office was located. In the lab setting, each couple was asked to use their "new" or "different" conflict management strategies that they had discussed during the interview session to resolve a *recent* conflict they experienced. A camera was placed in a nonintrusive spot and videotaped their conversation. I was in the "observer" room, where I could see the couple's activities through a one-way mirror.

I adopted a qualitative discourse analysis (Lupton, 1992) method to interpret data. This method involves intensive listening to audiotaped conversations, watching videotaped conversations, and reviewing the transcripts of these conversations. This process was guided by a theoretical lens on problematic integration. In particular, I referred to the Problematic Integration theory (or PI theory, Babrow, 1992, 1995, 2001, 2007) as a guiding framework to identify the analytical categories that help explain the root causes of participants' conflict experience.

During this process, each time a new piece of information emerged, I compared the incoming information to the original categories and decided whether to start a new theme or to add it to the original theme as a subcategory. Over the course of this analysis, I was mindful of allowing the themes to emerge naturally and understanding them without judgment. Moreover, I repeatedly returned to the data, examining whether the themes that developed accurately spoke to participants' experience as embedded in their words and the contexts associated with their responses.

PI theory offers a theoretical perspective on the relationship between communication, mind, and meaning. The goal of the analysis, however, is not to test PI theory but rather to use its concepts to illustrate how couples give meanings to their actions. After examining the underlying reasons of why "you can never see the world in the way I do," this chapter engages the readers to explore the possibilities of gaining perspectives of the other's view based on the themes emerged from couples' discussions of their conflict experience. Finally, this chapter presents key themes of dynamic verbal and nonverbal interactions as couples sought to "redo" their conflict during the interview session. Therefore, the goal of the data analysis is to illuminate and refine our understanding of the perspective-gaining process in the AIM proposed in chapter 2.

To protect participants' identity, pseudonyms are used to refer to their responses in the following analyses. Findings are summarized into two major categories with a series of themes under each category. The two major categories are labeled as (1) new insights and (2) lessons being learned.

Representative cases are based on real-life conflict experiences from six couples: Michelle and Tom (married for over 25 years), Paige and Ryan (girlfriend and boyfriend), Sarah and Ed (married for a few years), Erin and Jack (girlfriend and boyfriend), Britney and Chris (recently broke up), and Ling and Pete (newlyweds).

NEW INSIGHT I: UNCOVERING PROBABILISTIC EXPECTATIONS

A common theme in couples' discussions is their ongoing efforts to make sense of the other's mindset. One source of frustration is the "why" question in the sense that "why don't you see the problem in the way as I see it?"

According to PI theory (Babrow, 1992, 1995, 2001, 2007), humans form probabilistic and evaluative orientations to their experiences. Individuals' knowledge, beliefs, expectations, and the like form the basis for the probabilistic orientations with varying levels of assurance, certainty, or probability. Additionally, individuals evaluate these understandings in a positive or negative way. PI theory holds that our meaning-making behavior arises in these two deeply interrelated senses. In the context of conflict management, romantic couples clash on these two experiential orientations. They are largely unaware that the other party (he or she) sees the same conflict situation in a different probabilistic dimension or a different appraisal angle as positive or negative.

As you read the following illustrative example, focus on how Tom revealed his reasons for disapproving Michelle's spending habits, which is different from what Michelle thought about. In other words, their orientations toward meaning formation ("spending money") did not overlap.

Tom hesitated momentarily when asked if he could recall a recent conflict, and then replied, "The only thing I can think of is our money . . . and then you tell me it's your money and that you can do whatever you want to with it." His wife, Michelle, asked, "Oh, you mean how you said 'No' to me about spending?"

Tom went on to say, "I mean I ask what you spend it on. I bring up why she spends money on this and on that . . . and if she really needs it. And she gets mad and says, 'Well, I can buy whatever I want to buy.'"

When asked what he was thinking in mind, Tom said, "She always wants to do all these other stuffs that we never have money to do. So, I just forget it. . . . But I just want her to know that I don't think [you're spending on] it's on good stuff."

After having gained his perspective on spending on "good stuff," Michelle seemed to begin to feel better in that Tom cared about her wistful longing and remembered all those "other stuffs" that she wished to buy but could not afford. Also notice how the couple began to realize that they did not make their points clear enough in their first round of conflict talk (e.g., untold feelings and concerns).

Michelle: I didn't realize I was being so blunt or whatever about it. I do feel like I make good money and I should be able to spend money within reason. Saying it like, "Oh well, too bad! I don't care what you think." I don't mean it. Probably I didn't make it clear to him that I needed a right for spending money because I do work, too.

Later during the interview, Tom revealed that he chose to be quiet in order to calm her down. Michelle started to appreciate Tom's behavior rather than defending her spending habit.

Michelle: This is a good idea. You know, I think there are two ways that I could have approached it. If he had expressed to me what he just said, I would feel better. But he knows that I get very reactive and he probably didn't want to say anything more to get me more mad. So he just let it go. Would you say that's about right?
Tom: Yes . . . whether it's worth the argument or not.

This couple has been married for over 25 years. They already knew each other's conflict styles (e.g., reactive versus avoiding). But they never had a conversation like this before. Through a turn-taking procedure to express their concerns (e.g., "I thought," "I felt"), the couple began to realize that they hold two different perspectives on a conflict. Michelle focuses on the current episode as it is in the now, whereas Tom focuses more on the long-term consequence and their long-term purchase goals ("the good stuff"). Their evaluative orientations are different. Tom's evaluative orientation is on what counts as wise spending in the long run. For Michelle, on the other hand, buying things she likes is the focal point of her evaluative orientations. Hence, Tom's question of "what do you spend on?" is seen by Michelle as infringing upon her own right for spending.

They have never shared with each other their expectation-related differences until the interview session. One reason is that Michelle is reactive and emotional, so Tom always chooses to be quiet in order to calm her down. This part of finding suggests that critical to the formation of mutual understanding is the emergence of new awareness. In other words, discovering underlying causes of conflict that may be largely unknown in a relationship can be helpful. As illustrated in this couple's interview, Michelle and Tom disclosed their real intent explicitly for the first time. They indicated that neither of them has expressed their underlying frustrations of the conflict until the interview session.

This part of the finding also suggests that it is critical to establish a communication channel to allow each other to reveal one's original intent for action. Such communication channels include, but are not limited to, face-to-face conversation, writing a note to the other, or leaving a voice message. Such exchanges do not have to be done in a "once-and-for-all" manner. Rather, they should be part and parcel of the argumentative interaction process. Understanding each other provides a sense of relief. As Michelle put it, "I feel better after you told me this."

NEW INSIGHT II: CONTEXT AS SITUATED VERSUS EVOLVING

Not only did couples interpret conflict differently, they also handled it differently. Participants in the interview expressed diverse perspectives on how to respond to a conflict. If we imagine in our mind a conflict-formation continuum, participants' views can be located somewhere on the continuum. Let's identify one end of the continuum as exhibiting the idea that "conflict is a process; hence, it needs to be monitored" and the other end as "conflict is a product; it can be fixed right then and there." First, let's examine the following representative examples from Paige and Ryan as they describe their ways to react to a conflict. Using Ryan's words, "Communication is a huge battle in everyone's relationship, especially in our relationship."

Ryan: If we are in a bad mood, she will allow the bad mood to ruin her entire evening. At 6 o'clock she got [into] a scuffle with me. She sat on my stairs for an hour and would not talk. For me the scuffle is over. Let's get over it, for example, watch a movie together. I still love you and let's be happy.
Paige: (Laughter) Sounds like I'm crazy!

As table 6.1 illustrates, it is evident that one party has chosen a more active approach to eliminate the conflict, whereas the other party can live the conflict until it is out of control. However, if we look deeper into their different approaches, we may notice that they use "context cues" very differently when they perceive a conflict.

Using PI theory's terms, Paige and Ryan adopt different probable structure and meaning to perceive a conflict situation. The underlying cause of their different conflict approaches may relate to how they perceive a context. For

Table 6.1. Examples of Process versus Product Analogy to Conflict

General View	Examples	
	Paige's Narratives	Ryan's Narratives
Conflict is evolving	I usually let things build up . . . Then one thing happens, and it would set me off and freak me out. It could be something that wasn't a big deal. But because of all other stuff, it makes me freak out.	
Conflict should be eliminated		I discuss things to eliminate the problem. But she [Paige] shuts down and harbors it all. When we have a problem, I want to talk about it.

Paige, it is not about evaluating the current specific case; rather, it's about the process as a problem emerges, evolves, and how it builds up. She sees things as evolving over a period of time. But for Ryan, it is about the present moment; he likes to address and to eliminate the current problem, then move on.

According to PI, every conflict episode is a situated experience in the present moment, and it is also evolving, relating to past events that lead to the current and the future state of the relationship. Therefore, conflict formation is both a dynamic process and an outcome. The dynamism is particularly evident when the two parties in a conflict are unable to perceive each other's contextual picture of the problem. The following excerpt illustrates how Ryan and Paige pick up contextual information differently:

Ryan: I can recall a time just last week when we were casually hanging out. It was a fine night . . . and uhh . . . just the way her tone sometimes comes off very atittudey because she gets defensive about her hometown. She gets really defensive about the things that she really loves. I'm sure she would get defensive if someone is talking about me. So the problem with that is, when she gets defensive, it makes me feel defensive because I wish that she wouldn't feel that way. When I get defensive it makes my voice gets louder, and she gets upset because she feels that I am yelling at her.
Interviewer: Okay so what's your opinion on this?
Paige: Umm . . . the situation was . . . I'm really, really close to my family, and he was like, "Why do you have to go home so early?" So, of course, I took it as offensive and I said, "Because that's my home, you know." Probably I feel the whole reason it started was because he was rude about me going home. He

talked about it all day . . . how I was getting to Somerset, when I was leaving . . . stuff like that. It was just very annoying.

And then there's another thing . . . Oh, he yells at me. I've never had a guy yell at me or cuss towards me whatsoever, and he yells at me and cusses towards me. It really irritates me and makes me angry.

Interviewer: Okay. It's actually funny because you both actually have different perspectives of the same argument.

Ryan: Absolutely (*laughter*).

Despite all their disagreements, I could sense that Paige and Ryan are in love; their laughter, gentle touch, and affectionate look at the other party reveal their affection. While being cheerful, they expressed their struggles on how to "redo" the conflict for the better. They said they do not know what else they could do.

A similar struggle exists in Ed and Sarah's marriage. They have their own children, but they also live with 14-year-old Charlie, who is Ed's son from his previous marriage. According to Sarah, their conflict is over Charlie's "obviously intentional and inappropriate" behavioral problems. In their interview, Ed tried to bring two pieces of contextual information to Sarah's attention: (1) he is 43 years old and has a habit of avoiding conflict and (2) Charlie's living environment is different from their other kids. Charlie also lives with his biological mom occasionally. Here is how Ed and Sarah described their conflict:

Ed: I can remember a couple of instances that we've had conflict. But I don't believe it truly hurt. It probably left some small scars on the memory of what was said. But nothing severe. The argument started over my 14-year-old son who lives with us. He is not Sarah's son; Charlie is her step-son. I guess we have many disagreements about his behavior. And it got quite escalated when we discussed the boy's behavior.

Sarah: That's really about the only thing that we argue about. He always makes an excuse for him . . . and that's the main thing that keeps on building up . . . because I feel a lot of the times you can tell that what he's doing has a direct purpose. He's doing it intentionally and it's very easy for me to see but hard for him to understand.

Ed went on to emphasize the inconsistency of Charlie to live in a two-family environment, "You do have to remember one thing. He is steered away by his grandparents and mom, which his mom has restricted time with him." While Ed focuses on the underlying cause that plausibly explains Charlie's behavioral problem, Sarah emphasizes addressing issues that become problematic. As discussed previously, a conflict can be seen as both a process and an outcome. Therefore, Ed and Sarah's perspectives both hold some merit.

86   Chapter 6

When asked what they would do differently if they could turn back the clock and redo their interaction, they said the following:

Sarah: Probably to try and not let things build up and try and talk about it as soon as it happens vs. letting it build up and then explode.
Ed: Yes, but I'm 43 years old and I've dealt with conflict like that most of my life. I've let stuff build up. Sometimes I'll handle it; most times not. Most times I'll let it get to where I can't handle it any longer.
Sarah: Just maybe if we talked it through and came up with a better solution.
Ed: Yes, and then not speaking for some time about these things (*laughter*).

In these and many other ways, conflict is seen not only as still pictures of the current moment but also as a moving picture that is in its context. Couples expressed their diverging views of a situation. Through soliciting each other's views, couples realized that their views are subject to the vagaries of changing contexts. Although disagreements can never get completely settled, most couples in the interview eventually reached some sense of resonance and relief after openly discussing their views.

NEW INSIGHT III: THE COMFORT IN RELATIONSHIP

We have the impression that if people are in a good relationship, they should feel free to share feelings and concerns. But we may overlook the downside of feeling comfortable when speaking spontaneously. A third theme that emerged from the interview data is the different views on the level of comfort in addressing each other. On the one hand, it is the unbounded comfort in communication that may lead to conflict escalation. On the other hand, it is the confidence-based comfort that opens up communication with each other. Britney illustrated the former type of comfort in the following way:

> I used to wait and tell. But now I think it's a lot easier. I think that's what every couple really has a problem with. As you become comfortable with someone, you just act the way you think like whatever. Nothing that we've fought about has actually really been that important. It's just been a little fight that turns into a disaster over nothing. So, I think there's a better way to handle it.

Britney and Chris broke up a few weeks ago. They signed up for the interview because they wanted to understand why their relationship ended in a breakup. During the interview, Britney indicated that as they got deeper into the relationship, she felt more comfortable to respond more immediately, hence being her true "self." Chris, on the other hand, thinks comfort means confidence, knowing the "right" way to say things. According to him:

> As the relationship goes on, I guess you are more aware of what to say and what not to say. So, it's a better thing as the relationship goes on you can communicate more. Like I said we're like the same person. We know what gets under our skin. But I do have a filter . . . like I know when I'm going too far.

To a certain extent, Chris's definition of comfort in relational communication refers to more certainty in communication effect, rather than endorsing unguarded or carefree expressions. A clear message across these interviews seems to be this: "You can never see the world in the way I do." Frequently, couples assume they are thinking alike, but they never ask a question to check for sure: "Are you thinking what I'm thinking?" As an interviewer, I served as a moderator, asking each party to explain what he or she was both thinking and feeling in the conflict. It was at that critical moment that couples started to confront each other's perspective; they discovered they were arguing all the time while they were actually comparing apples and oranges.

Inspired by these couples' reflections on what they would do better if they could turn back the clock, the following section reports the lessons they learned.

LESSON I: OVERCOMING THE IMPULSE TO REACT IMMEDIATELY

Interview data suggest that each individual's underlying expectations and associated meaning construction of a situation are unknown to the other. Hence, it is almost impossible to understand exactly how the other sees the situation without explicitly checking with each other. Therefore, the first important lesson learned is that partners have to overcome the impulse of instantly responding to the other. Rather, they need to check their perceptions.

For example, in Michelle and Tom's interview, they recalled another conflict in which they planned a short vacation to allow them to spend some quality time together. Michelle wanted to visit another couple, but Tom said "No." It ended up with the wife driving to visit the couple 10 miles away, leaving her husband to stay in the hotel.

The husband's perspective was, "It takes away the whole purpose of the trip. We came up here to be together for the whole weekend. The other couple lives 10 miles away. It wasn't worth it." The wife responded as follows, which illustrates her spontaneous reaction:

Michelle: I would feel better if you explained the situation. I just jumped on the fact that he never wants to do anything; that he's not as social; and that's just the way he is. And it frustrates me even though I have to accept that. If he had expressed to me what he said, it would make me look at it differently.

During this interview, the more they exchanged their views, the more they appeared to appreciate their differences better. Here is what they said:

Michelle: I have a tendency to react with my feelings. I'm very reactive. When he says something, he stops and thinks. So I guess he really complements me well in this area.
Tom: I agree.

As readers, do you see the converging actions Michelle and Tom take in appreciating their differences? Michelle started to appreciate their differences, saying that he "complements me well in this area"; whereas Tom used a parsimonious expression of confirmation, saying "I agree."

Taken together, the first lesson is about inhibiting the instinct to react immediately. Instead of being reactive, ask a few questions to get the conversation moving: "Oh, I agree that it will take a lot of time to visit them. How about we call them and talk on the phone? What do you think of that?" "Will it be a good idea if we drive halfway, and meet them somewhere in the middle?" These kinds of open-ended questions trigger curiosity, possibly motivating each other to exchange perspectives. By gaining perspectives, rather than jumping to conclusions, couples gain more pathways for a smooth argumentative interaction.

LESSON II: APPRECIATIVE EXPRESSIONS ARE THE DRIVING FORCE

The mundane but powerful words, such as "This is an interesting thought" or "Yeah, I see your point," are necessary and relevant for couples' positive coping with their conflict. One noticeable action that emerged in the interviews is how couples express their affection in nonverbal channels in a broad sense of laughing, nodding, an affectionate look, or a gentle touch. Also evident in these conversations is the overt expression of "you never told me that" or "I agree." These expressions serve as the "attraction" mechanism that drives the disagreeing individuals in the converging direction. Sometimes it is an expression of humor that softens the tone. One participant said, "You are just like a turtle. That drives me crazy." The other responds, "You keep peeking at me and I close."

In the context of close relationship conflict, when any immediate solution is elusive, romantic partners are likely to feel frustrated or angry. In this kind of situation, verbal expressions of "I understand" and "You're right" seem to work as a tension-reducer. In the following illustrative example, Jack and Erin are graduating seniors. Erin thought that Jack did not listen to what she said.

Erin: It makes me feel like, you are tired of listening to me. You hear it, but you don't listen. It's frustrating.
Jack: When you say something, it puts an idea in my brain. It's not that I've stopped listening. It's I'm developing ideas in my brain.
Erin: You never told me that! I didn't know.

Later in the conversation, Jack indicated that Erin should be more considerate of how her decisions would affect the other.

Jack: Try putting yourself in the other's shoes. You don't think of how your thought or plan of action will affect me. In my brain, I think of every possible outcome. On the opposite, you outstrike the room and wonder, "How have I been getting out?"
Erin: (*Laughter*). Yeah, I know. It's not that I'm selfish. I don't think about it. It doesn't cross my mind. So. . . . How do we fix that?
Jack: I need to work on the train of thoughts in my brain.
Erin: And I need to work on how things will affect us. Fist bump! (*They bumped fists as a sign of celebration*)

In this case, the "fist bump" signifies mutual support and a celebration of their new understanding of each other. Appreciative expressions, either verbal or nonverbal, are essential in conflict talk. It is the motivating force to keep the conversation going. It signals interests and an invitation to the other party to join the conversation for problem-solving.

LESSON III: TACKLING THE PROBLEM—FINDING AN EXTERNAL FOCAL POINT

As couples reflected upon their problematic formulations of a conflict experience, an interesting cognition reconstruction phenomenon surfaced in this study. That is, as the discussion goes, couples tend to reshape their cognitions from my-view versus your-view to a view on how to tackle the problem itself. Therefore, couples refocus their attention to the problem itself rather than on finding fault with each other. Communication serves as a mechanism to generate, convey, and shape difficulties in new, novel ways. I call it cocreating an external focal point through communication (see also Babrow, 1992). That is, couples shift attention from the person who seemingly causes the frustration to the problem itself. For example, see the following example of Britney and Chris on the idea of pride:

Chris: Well, really, a big issue or part of it is pride. One wants to be more dominant than the other. And one is right and the other is wrong. It's like resolutions are sometimes hard to get because of this. I guess we need to work on the "pride" thing.
Britney: Yeah, even if you are not even mad anymore, your pride won't let you get down sometimes. You'll be arguing up the walls for nothing basically because of your pride. Yeah, the "pride" is an issue in our relationship.

In Erin and Jack's interview, they expressed that they liked the interviewer being behind an observatory mirror. They found that "imagining" someone watching them was helpful.

Erin: Maybe we should do this more. We need to sit down and talk about this. It feels much better. . . . . We can pretend that someone is watching us. Then we can talk.
Jack: We are doing very well because you (interviewer) are staring at us.

The phenomenon of creating an "external focal point" corresponds well to the "externalizing conversation" method in counseling psychology. According to Sommers-Flanagan and Sommers-Flanagan (2018), people in conflict have a natural tendency to blame either themselves or the other party when things go wrong. The externalizing therapy is used to help couples disassociate themselves from the problem, directing them to push the problem outside of their dispute realm. For example, a therapist can ask, "How does this issue bother your relationship?" By encouraging the couples to look at the problem from a distance, it takes away the pressure of accountability; hence, it reduces a defensive response.

Like the "externalizing conversation" method, couples in the present study have gradually externalized their conflict and defined it as a problem or a situation to deal with, for example, the issue of "pride" or a "watching eye." They utilize this creation to focus on their problem resolution, which permits them to alienate the emotional tensions inflicted by blaming each other.

LESSON IV: COMMITTING TO CLOSURE

A theme that constantly emerged from couples' reflections is the need to commit to closure. Closure, or the need for closure, refers to an individual's innate desire to get an answer on a given topic or inquiry (Roets et al., 2015). For example, in the context of conflict, when one asks a question or initiates an inquiry, she or he looks for a response from the other party. If one does not get an answer, he or she may feel uneasy about the other person, and that uneasiness can extend to the relationship as well. Why? Because a closure of the current topic provides some sense of certainty that an interpersonal problem is recognized as worthy of consideration. Couples mentioned that they need to explicitly tell the other person that they will provide a closure to the current problem.

A short-term commitment refers to an immediate response that signals engagement: for example, "Yes, I see what you mean" and "Let me think a little bit. I will let you know my take on it once I've cooled down a little bit." A long-term commitment refers to an effort to search more intensely for solutions through actions. Both commitments are needed in a conflict situation. For example, participants explained that they wish the other party could say a few words to explain his or her mindset rather than being still and silent. They wish the other party could show some gestures for relational assurance, such as "I don't know it at this moment, but we will talk through this little by little."

Roets et al. (2015) explained that the need for closure is the underlying motivational mechanism of the human mind and that it gives rise to knowledge inquiry, judgment, and decision-making. In conflict situations, when one party raises a concern and asks the other party to respond, a major source of emotional frustration is unleashed if the second party displays ambivalence, responds ambiguously, or ignores the message completely. As one couple mentioned, "If we say we will change, we need to change. If we never change, it is frustration." In this regard, walking away or being quiet are seen as dismissive gestures. Rather, expressions such as "I see your point. So how do we change? What should we do next?" serve the purpose of addressing the other party's fundamental need for closure.

In this regard, Ling and Pete's conflict reconstruction conversation serves as a good example. Both are college students and were recently married. Their conflict centered on a decision they had to make daily: what to cook for dinner. Ling cooked Chinese food and Pete did not like eating Chinese food for every meal. Ling agreed to learn more American cooking, and Pete then offered to cook some meals each week. Rather than complaining, they generated a compromise to address their issues at hand pretty efficiently.

The following "money" conflict illustrates their approach even more vividly. When you read their conversation, pay attention to Ling's expression of her burden ("I had too much in my thoughts and finally broke up") and how Pete responded with his "immediate solutions" (e.g., "working more," "We are not behind bills"). Observe the clues of how they address each other's need for closure.

Ling: Money seems to be an issue for us, especially because we just got married. We don't have a strong financial foundation. But we are young and still building it. I feel pressured this semester particularly, because I both work and study. I feel it is not fair to say that you don't work enough. I didn't want to bring up before. I had too much in my thoughts and finally broke up. In my heart, it's complaining. Rationally I think it is not your fault. It's your last semester. You should work hard on your last semester.

Pete: An immediate solution would be I work more now. But with student-teaching in the spring, basically it's a full-time job for free. I mean perhaps I can work at nights if I don't have to grade papers or do lesson planning for the next day. Or weekends. But you don't want me to do that because you would say, "I would not be at home enough." So what to do? (*Pete threw out a Chinese phrase "what to do" in his American accent. Ling laughed.*)

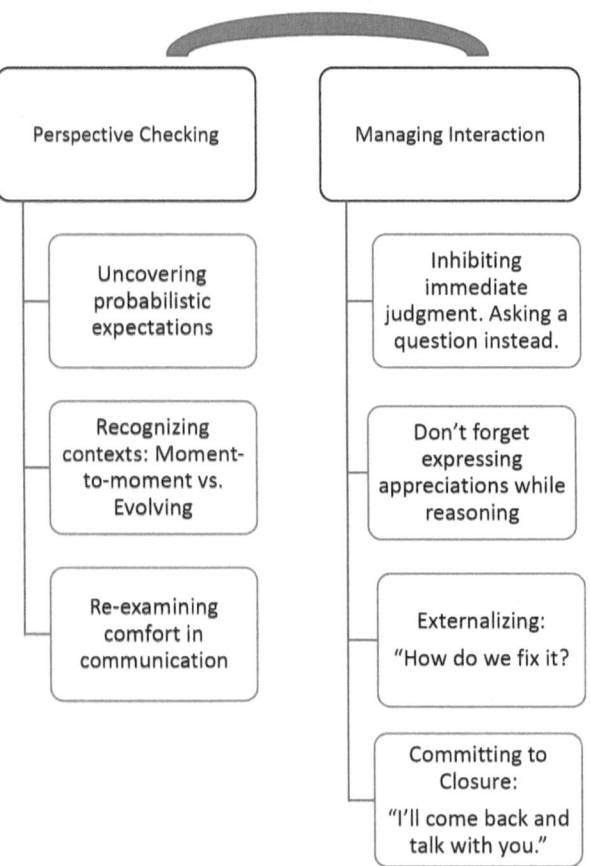

Figure 6.1. Key Concepts on Perspective-Taking Process and Conflict Interaction Management.

Ling: Maybe next semester when I will work less, I will feel more free. I won't give you as much burden as I'm going to myself now.
Pete: It's not that I choose not to work. I mean, I am going to work after I graduate in May. I will try to work as much as I can now.
Ling: (*Laughter*) So the solution would be "not to worry too much!"
Peter: Yeah, it's not like we are starving or behind on bills.
Ling: Nodding. Smiling.

What clues did you detect in their conversation that signal a commitment to addressing each other's need for closure? I found it interesting that Ling offered an immediate solution on her own: "Not to worry too much!" Although they could not resolve their financial problems immediately, they give each other a positive response and some measure of comfort.

In summary, a tentative response ("Let me think about it, but I promise I will get back with you") or a long-term commitment to get the conflict resolved serves the purpose to generate a closure to the issue at hand. In this sense, commitment to closure serves a similar function as punctuation in a sentence. It lets people know where we are in a communication chain of actions, whether it is a comma or a period.

The main themes illustrated in the preceding sessions are summarized in figure 6.1. The theoretical and practical implications of these findings are discussed in the following conclusion section.

CONCLUSION

We may fall in love at first sight, but we can rarely resolve a conflict in one shot. In this chapter, couples in my interview offered their insights on how to make a conflict experience more positive if they could turn back the clock and "redo" it. The findings of this study provide initial evidence that appreciation-oriented alternating communication process is not only possible to achieve but also conducive to joint problem-solving. Note that the appreciation-oriented alternating communication process did not occur during their original conflict episodes. This process occurred during the interview sessions when couples were asked to express their original intent to each other and seek to "redo" their conflict. This part of the finding suggests that what comes as easy and natural way to deal with conflict may not be the best approach. Rather, argumentative interactions need to be managed with measured steps and concerted effort.

In particular, this study offers a detailed illustration of the specific actions that couples take when they successfully "redo" their conflict, including the following: (1) Overcoming the instinct to respond immediately, checking perceptions first. (2) Expressing a positive regard to the other. During arguing, don't forget to show appreciative gestures to each other; hence, forge a bond and lighten up the atmosphere with attraction. (3) Pushing the interpersonal problem outside of the relational domain by collectively creating an external focal point. (4) Remembering to provide a closure expression to the other, letting the other person know that you are engaged in this problem-solving process.

What is the new knowledge gained through this research? This research highlights the key role of interaction management (i.e., perspective-gaining, alternating process) during argumentative interactions. That is, consistent with the AIM framework, this study illuminates that managing the flow of verbal and nonverbal interactions essentially serves as the conduit for the co-construction of social meanings. Without managing interactions (e.g., turn-taking, perception checking, affection expressions), communicators are more likely to reply on their intuitive reactions to deal with conflict as observed in the interview data in this study.

Since the initial establishment of the interpersonal communication discipline in the 1960s, communication theorists have never ceased from exploring the key components and processes of conflict management. For example, Coordinated Management of Meaning Theory by Pearce and his colleagues (1976, 1980, 2000) explained that individuals in a conversation co-construct their social realities. As such, a key to conflict management is to gain an understanding of how people employ various rules to construct and coordinate meanings in a conversation. The present study extends this theoretical perspective by clarifying that managing interaction flows (or alternating process) serves as a platform (or a conduit) for meaning coordination.

Furthermore, this study has identified three distinct causes that lead to divergent views in a conflict situation. To gain perspectives of the other's original intents and message choices, this research finds that it is important to ask at least three types of questions, including expectation inquiries (e.g., "In your mind, what counts as good and desirable?"), questions on the perceived context of the problem (i.e., conflict exists in the present moment versus evolving situation), and questions on each other's perceived certainty in a particular conflict situation (e.g., "What are you certain about?").

By highlighting the actions and process of gaining perspectives, the present study offers new insights on how couples take specific communicative actions to uncover each party's underlying needs and to motivate each other to participate in the conflict dialogues. Like what Baxter (1990, 2010) suggested in her relational dialectics theory, there are multiple, sometimes competing voices, desires, or forces centered on a relationship issue, and such tensions are always part of our relational life. To sustain a happy relationship, individuals need to recognize those changing needs on both sides of the tension. The findings of this research provide new details on how couples recognize and manage tensions in their relational life.

One important conclusion of this study is that perspective-taking does not happen easily. It takes several conversational exchanges. It occurs when couples actually invest time to immerse themselves in the conversational moments with their emotions being relatively calm and pleasant. As said previously, couples laugh and touch each other with affection. It is only when couples are willing and ready to consider the perspectives of the other that perspective-taking begins to occur.

The message is: Relational communication is full of unknown territories, so embrace the journey!

NOTES

1. The author wants to thank Haley Ferrell, an undergraduate from MTSU's Honors program, for her help during the interview data collection process.

2. The author wants to thank Chelsea Adams and Qwantilla Crawford, undergraduate students at MTSU, for transcribing couples' conversations and for coding data.

Chapter 7

Defusing Defenses and Speaking Skillfully

Steve Mortenson

Jenny and Danika just finished a diversity seminar at work. Jenny found it really interesting, but Danika was really put off by some things the facilitator said:

Danika: That whole thing was ridiculous! What are they talking about? White privilege!? I worked my ass off to get where I am! My whole family did; we never took a handout, we never asked for anything! There was no privilege involved; we worked hard like everyone else! But because I'm white, now I'm privileged?!

Jenny: I know, it sounds like they're saying you're a bad person; it's a really hard thing to have that leveled at you.

Danika: It is!

Jenny: It's not an easy thing to hear, especially if you come from a family with a work ethic like yours. And it's pretty clear that everyone here knows you go the extra mile. But I don't think they were saying we don't work hard. I understood white privilege as not having to put up with certain things. Like we've never been threatened or demeaned by racists based on our skin color. Right?

Danika: No—I know that.

Jenny: Right, we just don't have to worry about someone threatening or demeaning us at work or in public based on our race. That is one hassle that we don't have to deal with, while people of color have to deal with it all the time. So I think of white privilege as all the heartaches and hassles that we get to *avoid* and not even *think about*, while Black people have to put up with these issues constantly.

Danika: I guess so, but that doesn't make *us* racists.

Jenny: Not consciously, like I know we don't *consciously* have anything against Black people.

Danika: Of course not! I've got Black friends . . .

Jenny: Right, but both of us still fall into racial biases we're not aware of. It has to do with how we were raised. Look, I know it's not my fault I was raised with my biases or privilege, but I still have to do something about these views so they don't hurt people. Remember, the trainer said everyone has biases no matter what color we are; it's just part of being human. I don't want to be in an unfair workplace where people are discriminated against. I want everyone to have an equal shot at getting ahead and I know you want that too. Remember Bill?

Danika: Yeah, the guy who only promoted men.

Jenny: Exactly. Remember how much that sucked?

Danika: I remember.

Jenny: Well, that could be happening to all the people of color we work with right now and we don't even see it. I don't want that, and I don't think you do either. So remember that thing they talked about, the Implicit Attitude Test? I took it on my phone during the break and it really surprised me. Can I send you the link? I think you'll find it really interesting.

Danika: What does it show you?

Jenny: It shows biases you didn't know you had—for and against all kinds of different people.

Danika: And it showed you some of yours? Because I don't see you as a prejudiced person at all.

Jenny: Yeah, it did; it was really eye opening.

Danika: Well, I guess I'll try that. Send me the link.

Helping someone acknowledge their biases is difficult and usually takes more than one conversation. It is pretty clear that Danika is really threatened by the diversity training and fell into what Robin DeAngelo (2018) has termed white fragility. White fragility occurs when even a minimum amount of racial stress becomes intolerable and triggers a range of defensive emotions such as anger, fear, and guilt, and behaviors including argumentation, silence, and leaving the stress-inducing situation. Danika's reaction to the term "white privilege" is understandable given that white privilege is largely invisible to white people. Part of the privilege is not realizing that one possesses such privilege in order to avoid feelings of guilt due to benefitting from the unfairness of one's culture and history (McIntosh, 2004).

Nonetheless, Jenny was able to effectively manage Danika's defensiveness by supporting her and offering understanding. By validating (rather than challenging) a target person's upset feelings and by supporting their self-image, we are able to help others in emotional distress open up to perspective taking and advice during emotionally upsetting episodes (Burleson & Goldsmith, 1997). Trying to force perspective taking on someone while they are still in emotional distress is generally ineffective and results in more emotional upset (Goldsmith, 2004). It is also beneficial to let a target person know that we understand the challenge or struggle he/she is going through when offering advice or corrections (Goldsmith, 2004; MacGeorge et al., 2016). Jenny's ability to confront and advise Danika supportively helped Danika not to feel judged by her reactions and helped her think more about how she too was the victim of biased behaviors. By working to defuse Danika's defenses, Jenny was able to keep Danika open to learning more about racism and her place in it.

Supportive confrontation is all about defusing defenses, both our own and others. In chapter 3, I discussed how the Strengths and Shadows Deep Personality Assessment helps learners to identify their shadows and the kinds of things they project onto others. In this chapter, I will describe in more detail how to defuse four different types of shadow projections. I will then present some supportive message strategies and highlight some of their key features. Finally, I will present an exploratory, qualitative analysis of supportive confrontation reports given by students in a cocurricular leadership program to illustrate the different ways that people deploy supportive confrontation strategies. First, let's revisit the problem of bias from some other angles, namely, from white privilege, colorism, and benevolent prejudice.

White Privilege and Colorism

When we talk about racial discrimination in the United States, the discussion generally focuses on the all too real disparities between white people against black people or other people of color. The concept of *white privilege* is used to describe all the unearned assets and protections that white people enjoy due to their skin color and position in cultures permeated with white supremacy. Some specific examples of white privilege include the ability to be in the company of people of your race most of the time, being able to shop or be in public without fear of harassment due to your skin color, and assuming that your neighbors will either be neutral or pleasant to you (McIntosh, 2004). It is difficult to persuade people to acknowledge their white privilege. No one wants to see themselves as spoiled or privileged or the beneficiary of racism and injustice. Thus, people confronted with their privilege often display intense anger, tearful anguish, or anxious rationalizations about why they are "not racist" (DiAngelo, 2011).

Even more difficult to acknowledge is the system of white supremacy that provides those privileges. Acknowledging white supremacy as the source of our privilege implicates us in all of the brutal injustices of contemporary racism and the traumatic history of our country (Leonardo, 2004). If we possess white privilege, we want to believe we can counteract our privilege individually by being kind, compassionate, respectful, and fair with the individual people of color with whom we interact. While such behavior is often appreciated at the personal level, it is still inadequate (McIntosh, 2004). If we possess white privilege and truly wish to counter or neutralize such privilege, we must also address and work to change the larger cultural systems in our families and communities that perpetuate white supremacy. In other words, it is not enough to say that I am "not racist" and that I, as an individual, treat people equitably. If I truly care about racial equity and inclusion, then I must actively work to correct and remove concepts, policies, practices, and laws that perpetuate white supremacy. Anything less is an attempt to comfort myself without doing the necessary and difficult work to achieve social justice for people of color.

Less widely discussed is the concept of *colorism* (or light privilege) which involves the allocation of privilege and disadvantage based on skin color, with a prejudice for lighter skin. Said differently, colorism distributes privilege and discrimination along a continuum of skin tones with the darkest-hued people suffering the most discrimination and hardship and the lighter- and lightest-hued people reaping the greatest amounts of unearned benefits. Victims of colorism not only suffer through greater economic, social, and health hardships than the lighter-skinned people of color in their communities, they also endure discrimination from lighter-skinned people of color. Said differently, lighter-hued people of color commit and perpetuate color discrimination against darker-hued people of color. In the United States, researchers report significant levels of colorism within Black and Latinx communities (Hochschild & Weaver, 2007; Hughes & Hertel, 1990; Keith & Herring, 1991; Seltzer & Smith, 1991).

Gender plays a critical role in colorism. Darker-hued women experience more colorism than darker-hued men of color. Moreover, these women also suffer greater losses in terms of health and employment, and they suffer social disadvantages related to finding marriage partners. Codes and concepts of beauty for women of color often exalt lighter skin tones and leave darker-hued women feeling unattractive and less valuable. For darker-hued women, colorism against them is often established and perpetuated by the lighter-hued women within their own families and then confirmed by their larger communities and the media (Conrad, Dixon, & Zhang, 2009; Maxwell, Abrams, & Belgrave, 2016).

Colorism, especially against women, is practiced across cultures in India (Vaid, 2009), China (Yeung, 2015), Indonesia (Saraswati, 2013), Japan (Arudou, 2013), Latin America (Flores & Telles, 2012), and Africa (Jablonski, 2012; Lewis et al., 2013). Many scholars point to the white supremacy and slave trade of Europe and America as the impetus for global colorism (Andrews, 2014; Knight, 2010; Monk, 2014; Norwood, 2013). Other scholars suggest that colorism in India and in East Asian countries comes from esthetic traditions related to classism. Darker-hued people were associated with poor laborers who worked in harsh sunlight while lighter-skinned people were associated with merchants and wealthy land owners who worked indoors (Dixon & Telles, 2017). In precolonial Africa, Arab slave traders established a colorist hierarchy that favored their lighter skin tones over the African people they sold as slaves (Jablonski, 2012; Lewis et al., 2013). Today, multinational corporations continue to perpetuate colorism and light supremacy in women and children across the world by marketing and selling skin bleach creams and other skin-lightening products (Hunter, 2007, 2011).

Research on colorism and implicit bias make it clear that racial discrimination is much more complex than oversimplified concepts like malicious white people knowingly oppressing people of color, who are themselves passive victims of discrimination. This is not to dismiss the preponderance of overt racism and conscious white supremacy that continues to thrive across the world but to add more nuanced and subtle forms of racism to our working knowledge. As we have seen, even well-meaning people who consciously ally themselves with people of color can fall into discriminatory thoughts and behaviors unconsciously. Also, racial discrimination is practiced by people of color against each other and practiced in other countries around the world. It is important to understand the larger global and historical picture of racism beyond our own national borders and history. Doing so broadens our understanding of what constitutes racism as well as who commits and perpetuates racial prejudice. Further, it illustrates that our own biases and discrimination are often allied with human tendencies toward cognitive mistakes and unconscious emotions.

Hopefully, conceptualizing these more subtle forms of racism as human error instead of human evil aids those of us who choose to face the dilemma of our own racism. For those of us with white or light skin privilege, it is daunting and difficult to acknowledge such privileges and what those factors mean in terms of our lives and sense of self. More daunting is to acknowledge that our continued receipt of privilege perpetuates our implication in the horrors and injustices of white supremacy. Understanding the global range, complex allocations of discrimination, and often unconscious nature of bias can help us to better counteract our own racism and help to dismantle the white supremacy of our culture. I will briefly describe a final concept of subtle discrimination that many well-intentioned people continue to perpetuate: benevolent prejudice.

THE CORROSIVE KINDNESS OF BENEVOLENT PREJUDICE

Like the implicit bias described in chapter 3, benevolent prejudice is subtle, hard to detect in ourselves, and challenging to call out in others. It is a kind of corrosive kindness where our good (but naive) intentions lead to negative outcomes, especially for women and people of color (Mortenson, 2017). While implicit bias is characterized by negative feelings of discomfort and anxiety, benevolent prejudice is marked by "flattering" emotions that support our self-images such as sympathy, amusement, or guilt toward a person from an underrepresented out-group (Fazio & Hilden, 2001; Fiske et al., 2002; Swim & Miller, 1999). There are many forms of benevolent prejudice in which we see people from different groups in a *positive but powerless light* and, as a result, fail to treat them equitably. For example, benevolent racism against black people stems from perceptions that they are not only social, athletic/creative, emotional, family oriented, good humored, economically deprived, and fun loving but also incompetent and irresponsible (Ramasubramanian & Oliver, 2007; Van den Berghe, 1978). Despite the good intentions of such feelings, they can be just as hurtful, offensive, and inappropriate as hostile prejudice (Swim & Stangor, 1998). Moreover, benevolent racism works to suppress policies geared toward addressing systematic discrimination (such as Affirmative Action) while enabling and supporting racist institutions such as racial profiling in law enforcement and opposition to gun control (Esposito & Romano, 2014). Benevolent prejudice also occurs as sexual discrimination as we'll see in this next dialogue.

Brooke was furious when she heard that Carl was not going to send Amy, a junior project leader, to lead and present the presentation she had produced. Brooke herself had been left out more than a few times because her male counterparts were afraid she could not handle the pressure and stress of various projects and company personnel. It angers her to see it happening to Amy. She wants to chew Carl out for being sexist but she recognizes that her anger is triggered by her own experiences of being patronized. She also knows that unlike some of the aggressively sexist men she has had to put up with, Carl genuinely respects and appreciates the women he works around. Brooke recognizes that projecting the shadow of her past predators onto him is neither fair nor effective.

Before she confronts Carl, she separates her feelings about her own experiences from what is happening now. She works through her anger at Carl and recognizes that Carl's sexism is more a cognitive error than a character flaw. Therefore, she decides on her goals for talking to Carl. She knows that making Carl defensive won't help him understand his biases nor would it help Amy professionally.

Brooke: Hi, Carl, I wanted to talk to you about who you're sending to do the presentation for the East Office.
Carl: I was going to send Henry and Wayne.

Brooke: Why not Amy? She did most of the analysis and she led the project team.
Carl: I know, and she did a great job, it's just—well, you know— East Office is pretty old school, and they can be kind of rough on women. I didn't want to put Amy through all that.
Brooke: I know, and I can tell your intentions are good here; you're trying to shield Amy from some of the harsher and more sexist personnel. I understand that, and I know you'd never consciously pass her over or shut her out of anything important. But at the same time, if Amy is going to grow professionally and take on more leadership responsibilities, she needs to show that she can handle situations like this. If we take her out of those situations, we could rob her of an opportunity to show what she is made of. So, your concern might help her avoid something unpleasant in the short term, but it may end up impairing her professional growth in the long run. I know you respect and appreciate her, and I'm confident you don't want that.
Carl: No, I really don't. I guess I thought I was doing her a favor.
Brooke: I realize that—and that's sort of the issue. We don't feel the need to protect Henry or Wayne because they're both guys, but because Amy is a young woman, we assume she needs protection. It's an unconscious, cultural thing, but we still have to catch ourselves or it will end up hurting Amy's career. The problem is if my biases are well intended, I don't see how I am impairing a person's professional growth. We need to assume Amy's as tough as the guys here and can handle the same challenges, or she won't live up to her career potential. And, to be frank, the guys in East Office need to wake up and get used to seeing women come in and lead.
Carl: Well, *that's* true enough—I guess it's hard for me to not want to watch out for her.
Brooke: I get that. You know, as a woman, I thought I couldn't have any gender biases against women, but then, I read this article on benevolent sexism and realized I have gender biases too. Can I send you this article? It was really interesting, and I think you'll find it helpful.

While Carl's good intentions and positive emotions toward Amy are sincere, they are also the foundation of his covert discrimination against her. Benevolent sexism is based on emotions like well-intentioned concern or appreciation that exaggerate the warmth or relational skills of women while devaluing their competence and leadership potential (Bosson et al., 2010). Benevolent sexism describes the implicit view that women are emotionally warm but incompetent, need to be protected from adversity, have social and domestic qualities that men do not possess, and serve to fulfill the emotional and romantic needs of men (Glick & Fiske, 1996, 2001). We can see in the dialogue how Carl unconsciously fell into a protector role with Amy instead of trusting her competence and ability to handle herself. It is important to note that enduring benevolent sexism can be worse than facing hostile sexism: benevolent sexism is just as emotionally damaging as hostile sexism. It affords women with fewer resources for coping and responding to discrimination, leads women to unwittingly confirm to gender stereotypes, and alters their self-perception in ways that impair their leadership and career aspirations (Bosson et al., 2010; Dardenne, Dumont, & Bollier, 2007; Good & Rudman, 2010; Jost & Kay, 2005).

One of Brooke's goals for her confrontation was to avoid projecting a hostile predator onto Carl. That meant she had to become clear about her feelings about her own past and how she viewed Carl in the present situation. Shadow projection is inherently emotional, so one fundamental challenge is discerning between appropriate and inappropriate emotional responses to another person's problematic behavior. In this next section, I will begin by discussing how to discern the emotions behind projection and then discuss how to defuse different types of shadow projection before a confrontation.

IDENTIFYING SHADOW TRIGGERS

One common question I hear when training or teaching about the shadow is this: How can I tell the difference between a real threat and a shadow trigger? Being triggered or activated is when we feel threatened without there being an actual threat. We suddenly feel angry, afraid, or guilty without questioning the logic behind these emotions. What is needed is the ability to discern appropriate emotional responses from reactive emotions tangled up in our pasts and then defuse those feelings by separating the past feelings from the present person (Richo, 2008).

Appropriate and Inappropriate Anger

Averill (2012) claims that appropriate anger requires an unjustified transgression against us, the ones we love, or the things we care about. Anger toward the transgression renders an aggressive response appropriate. In fact, aggression in response to a transgression is sometimes required if we are to keep the respect of others as well as our own self-esteem. The social/cultural function of anger is not to punish or hurt others but to correct their antisocial behavior: without an identifiable transgression, anger is merely aggression or cruelty (Averill, 2012).

Other research suggests that aggression is often the result of displaced fear and anxiety, especially when we feel under threat. In other words, the initial fear for our own safety is transformed into aggression against outsiders or people we perceive to be critical of us or our way of life (Arndt et al., 1997). For example, in the United States, one common aftermath of a terrorist bombing either at home or abroad is that ethnic Indian, Pakistani, Persian, and Arabic people in America (who had nothing to do with terrorism) are targeted and attacked by white Americans (Stack, 2015). In short, a good deal of our anger is actually fear wrapped up in an intimidating costume.

Given all this, when we are consumed with anger, an important tactic for recognizing projection is to identify the unjustified transgression against us. In other words, if I cannot identify the line someone has crossed with me, if I can find no discernible and unjustified transgression against me or mine, then my anger has no legitimacy and I have no right to hostility against the person setting me off. My shadow is activated by something in my past and I am most likely projecting a predator onto someone who lacks any aggressive intent against me.

It might also be that I cannot stop projecting on a person who has wronged me in the past. Even when this person is being sincere and benevolent, I project malicious intent taken from our shared history. In this case, the challenge is to realize there is no transgression during our interaction together and, thus, no reason to become defensive or aggressive. Finally, to put it candidly, there are a lot of emotionally unskillful people out there who are still held hostage by their difficult pasts; they are wounded, defensive, and angry, and their lack of emotional and social skills is a burden for everyone around them. It is easy to become activated and then project on such people, leading us to fall into our own defensive and aggressive shadows. Recognizing and defusing our projections helps us to differentiate between unconscious, unskillful behavior and actual, willful malevolence. When we defuse our projections, we can learn not to take someone's dysfunctional personality personally. To put it succinctly, activation equals aggression without transgression.

Appropriate and Inappropriate Guilt

Like anger, guilt also serves a social/cultural function; guilt encourages us to adhere to the moral and ethical guidelines of our society and relationships (Hoffman, 2013). We experience appropriate guilt when we have consciously and willfully broken an agreement we have made with ourselves or someone else. Feelings of guilt serve as the impetus to get us back into integrity with our values and ideals or back into fidelity with the person with whom we have broken trust (Richo, 2008).

Unfortunately, we also fall into inappropriate guilt. This happens when we have made no agreement with either ourselves or someone else, yet we still feel culpable for a negative outcome (Richo, 2008). For example, it is one thing to promise my friends a ride to the airport and then cancel on them at the last minute; now I am responsible for their bad outcome and should feel guilty. However, feeling guilty because I am unable to give them a ride in the first place is dysfunctional. Such an instance calls for sympathy or compassion for my friends and their situation, but unless I have made an explicit agreement to provide a ride, there is nothing to feel guilty about.

Inappropriate guilt is another emotion that activates shadow projection: we suddenly feel like a perpetrator and cast the other person as a victim through projection. Thus, another important tactic to defuse shadow projection is to recognize when we are feeling guilty without having made or broken an explicit agreement. If I am unable to identify the agreement I have made and broken with another person, I must tell myself that my guilt is unwarranted, and that sympathy or compassion are more appropriate feelings. To put it simply, projection equals guilt without an agreement made or broken.

Appropriate and Inappropriate Fear

Authentic and appropriate fear involves appraising some element or object in our environment as a threat to ourselves, our goals or ego, or the people and things we care about (Lazarus & Lazarus, 1994). The vital point here is that appropriate fear requires a fear object, some tangible or objective threat. For example, it is one thing to be confronted by a large and aggressive dog in an alley, and it is quite another to worry about aggressive dogs when I am safely at home with no threat of attack. This is the difference between fear and anxiety. Anxiety is a feeling of fear that lacks a distinct fear object. Feeling anxiety is about uncertain outcomes and all the worries we have about them. Fear relates to bad outcomes that are certain or highly probable; anxiety is worrying about what is simply possible without really considering the probability. When we appraise a situation or person with fear, it activates our fight or flight instincts. We either want to flee or confront the threat. Anxiety activates the same instincts but leaves us no way to act: we cannot confront or flee from the unknown. Anxiety is often about playing the "what if" game. A student version of "what if" goes something like this: *What if I don't get that internship and then I can't find a job and then I'm homeless and then I'm living under a bridge in a cardboard box eating cat food?*

Anxiety is a very common projection trigger. An important tactic for defusing it is to realize that our feelings have no discernible object, source, or cause other than our own memories about past traumas or victimization. When we can separate our fears of the past from what is happening at the moment, we can get hold of our anxiety, defuse our defenses, and better manage an activated shadow. In this next section, I will describe specific steps to defusing shadow triggers.

DEFUSING SHADOW TRIGGERS

Here are four concise steps to defusing a shadow trigger. When we suddenly realize that a shadow is activated and we are able to do the emotional work to defuse it, the anger, fear, or defensiveness literally falls away, and we are back in a calmer and more rational state of mind.

Step 1: Discern Your Emotions

Pay attention to sudden surges of fear, defensiveness, or aggression, especially around specific people. We can tell when we are triggered because our emotions are disproportionate to the situation: we are feeling too angry, too defensive, or too scared. The situation does not really warrant the intensity of how we feel. Try to observe your feelings but don't identify with them. Ask yourself what *exactly* is at risk here? Is this person or situation an actual threat? "Is someone doing something on purpose to me? Are they actually crossing a line or are they just being who they are anyway?" Does this situation have critical consequences worthy of my fear or anger? Or will I just "look bad"? Half the battle here is realizing that we are triggered and that our best course is to say and do nothing reactive at the moment. If you can sense that you need to express some of your triggered feelings, do it later in a safe space or with someone you trust. Don't indulge or repress feelings, express them skillfully and in ways that don't compromise you. Then, let them go.

Step 2: Identify Your Shadow

When you realize you're triggered, the next step is to identify what part of your shadow is activated. Look back into your past and you may recognize that a shadow from childhood is hijacking you now. Once you get a sense of where this shadow came from or who gave it to you, you can put it in the right context: it's an echo from your past that is distorting your present.

Step 3: Self-Talk

It may feel weird at first, but talk back to your feelings, ask them questions. We listen to our fears and doubts whispering to us all day long, so why not answer back? Ask your fear or anger, "What do want from me?" You may be surprised what you get back. Emotions are just information and, like information, they need to be acknowledged (felt) but not always acted upon. Call out your shadow: "This person is not out to get me; it's just my victim shadow getting sensitive again"; "This person won't hate me if I say no, it's just my wounded helping going off"; "My life is not a tarpit, it's just me getting restless again."

Step 4: Choose Your Behavior

Once you've identified the shadow that's triggered, identify it as part of your childhood or past and describe how it no longer fits into your adulthood. "That's just my people pleaser trying to make my parents happy, but now I'm a grown adult and I have to be honest and polite with people. I also know how to politely speak my mind. So. I'm going to say what I need to say here." "Okay, I'm falling into my know-it-all which is how I protected myself from criticism when I was a kid. But I don't need that approach anymore because I'm an adult and there's no threat here, just disagreement." If you get snared by fear—don't beat yourself up. Rather, talk to your fear as if it were a little child, comfort it, and tell it everything will be okay. In many ways, our shadows are children, especially when they come to us with fear. The best response then is to comfort them.

IDENTIFYING SHADOW PROJECTIONS

In chapter 3, I described the phenomena of shadow projection, the process in which we project some denied trait about ourselves onto another person and then condemn him or her for supposedly possessing or enacting it. Here are some questions to consider as we further explore shadow projection: Are there people in your life that just set you off without even meaning to? They just get under your skin without even doing anything to you and you become irritated and angry. What it is about them that sets you off? What is the behavior that gets to you? Are there people in your life that get away with things that make you angry? Do they do things that you would never consider doing, but the fact that they get away with it burns you up? What are these things and why do they make you angry? Are there people in your life that make you feel defensive? Even when they are being polite and considerate, you still feel judged. What is the judgment you feel is being held against you?

When we become cognizant of the triggers and "contents" of our projections, we are able to defuse our defensive attributions and feelings and enact more mindful and skillful responses (Hollis, 2008; Richo, 2008). Thankfully, it is a relatively straightforward process of reflection and identifying our projections and the types of people we target for projection. With that in mind, this next section identifies four different types of shadow projections and then summarizes strategies for defusing our projections (Mortenson, Luchey, & Creasy, 2015; Mortenson, 2017).

Identifying Projections of Self-Judgment

Have you ever met someone when you were new on the job or at school and you were just sure they disliked you? You went around thinking, "They hate me; I can tell they hate me." When you finally confronted the person and asked, "Why don't you like me?", he or she responded with, "I'm sorry, *who are you again?*" Or maybe you found out they know you, but have no problem with you at all, and that the criticism was literally *all in your head.* Here's another example: I was leaving a party during graduate school with a friend. Everyone was having a good time and seemed to be relaxed and festive. But as soon as my friend and I were out the door, my friend stomped and shouted:

"I'm just as smart as all those people!"
"What do you mean?" I asked, "Was someone talking trash to you?"
"No, no one said anything. I could just tell . . . they all think they're soooo brilliant."

At one time or another, we all feel judged, looked down on, and critiqued by people who have absolutely nothing against us. In other words, we project negative self-judgments about ourselves onto other people and then blame those individuals for judging us (when the real truth is that we are judging ourselves). This is another form of shadow projection. One method of raising awareness about this projection is to acknowledge when we project our own self-judgments onto others and then falsely accuse them of critiquing us.

In addition, we often attribute malicious intent to the unskilled behavior of others toward us; we decide people are dismissive with us because they think we are flakey or incompetent instead of simply being busy or overwhelmed themselves (Hollis, 2008; Richo, 2008). We decide people are short with us because they look down on us, not because they are having a bad day. Catching self-judgment reins in unnecessary anger and shows us glimpses of what we fear in ourselves and project onto others. Catching self-judgment may involve asking yourself: Where is the evidence that he or she feels this way?

Identifying Projections of Our Own Faults onto Others

Remember that person who sets you off without even meaning to? A useful strategy for understanding how we project our own flaws onto others is to identify people who bother or irritate us but never actually cross a line with us; they just "get under our skin." Often such people mirror some denied aspect of our own personality, such as arrogance, greed, incompetence, or laziness (Cramer, 2006). For example, we may see a colleague display a moment of bias or prejudice in a meeting. Observing that display activates the anxiety (and potential shame) we have around our own biases. We then dispel these unpleasant self-feelings by turning them into anger and aggressive judgments toward our target person. By projecting our "bigot" onto a colleague, we make our target person doubly biased: now they possess both their bias and ours. Further, in the future, we feel greater license to treat them poorly. Projection obscures our ability to relate to people objectively because we always see them as worse than they actually are (Cramer, 1998; Hollis, 2008). In contrast, if we can recognize and "own" our own capacity for bias instead of denying and projecting it onto others, we may realize, "My colleague is acting like a total bigot right now, and sometimes I have prejudiced thoughts and moments as well." Taking this strategy a step further entails first listening to all the "jerks" we put up with in life and all their negative traits, then assessing our own capacity for such traits, as well as the moments we have embodied the same negative traits. In short, owning what set us off helps us control our reactions.

Identifying a Predator/Victim Projection

Understanding the emotional dynamics of bullying can help us to better identify a predator/victim projection. Children who are bullied at home by parents or older siblings often deny their own powerlessness and victimhood by projecting it onto other more vulnerable children and then bullying them. When bullies see a weak or vulnerable child, it triggers their own feelings of fear and powerlessness and activates the defense. They project their own weakness onto a target child. Having transformed their fear into aggression, bullies turn predator and aggress on weaker children to further disavow their own feelings of powerlessness.

The victims of childhood bullying may not turn into childhood bullies themselves, but as adults, they are more likely to be triggered by adult acts of bullying, even when they are only bystanders or observers. In the same manner, the triggered victim transforms old fear into new aggression, turns predator, and "bullies" the bully with the same lack of skill or consciousness (Hollis, 2008; Mortenson, 2007). Given the hostility and bullying style of overt sexism and racism, it is reasonable to assume that girls and children of color who have suffered the demeaning shame of discrimination in their past are also likely to be triggered into unskillful aggression by incidents of bias during adulthood.

It is easy to project the bullies from our past onto the challenging people in our present and then become defensive and aggressive at the thought of being victimized again. In order to defuse the predator/victim projection, I have to consciously separate the past from the present. This requires a three-fold process. First, I have to withdraw the projection of whomever terrorized me in the past away from the person I am currently facing. I must remind myself of some vital facts: this is not the person who had the power to hurt or humiliate me as a child; this is someone else whose unskillful behavior has nothing to do with my past. Next, I have to move out of my victimhood and realize that, as an adult, I have more than enough skill and power to defend myself without becoming aggressive or defensive; I can hold and set boundaries with others. Lastly, if it is clear that *I am* facing a bully or witnessing predatory behavior, I need to remember that most bullies will quickly fold when stood up to calmly and rationally because their emotions are driven by their own fears of being powerless.

Identifying an Unmet Need Projection

One of the most difficult projections to identify is when we project our own unmet needs onto other people and then accuse them of doing something that we ourselves fear to do. The difficulty lies in our inability to admit to the need. However, I know I'm projecting an unmet need onto someone else when I feel *both* disapproval *and* envy about what he or she is doing. My ego publicly disapproves of the behavior, but my shadow secretly envies that person's ability to "get away with that." Recognizing this ambivalent mixture of disapproval and envy is key to defusing this kind of shadow projection. Consider all the times you may have said the following things to yourself:

I wish I could just blow the day off and go mess around.
I wish I could just shoot my mouth off and say whatever I want.
I wish I could just take care of myself for a change.

The tone may sound sarcastic, but part of us really does want these things. Here are some common unmet needs and shadow projections.

> If I'm afraid to ask for help—I'll project "neediness" onto someone who is not afraid to seek help.
> If I'm afraid or unable to relax—I'll project "slacker and lazy" onto people who can slow
> down and take it easy.
> If I'm afraid to speak up and assert myself—I'll project rude or belligerent behaviors onto people who freely speak their mind.

Remember those people in your life that always "get away" with things. Perhaps, what is so infuriating about them is that they are not afraid to do something we are still afraid to do. Defusing the projection of an unmet need occurs when we acknowledge the need and, then, when we find healthy ways to meet them. When we learn to stick up for ourselves, bullies become sad and pathetic. When we learn to take care of our own needs, selfish people appear isolated and lonely. Many times, as soon as we recognize we are projecting a need, anger and resentment falls away and is replaced with greater awareness.

DEFUSING SHADOW PROJECTIONS

When we encounter another person who shows us a part of our shadow, some unwanted trait we were shamed for or taught to suppress, we project that trait onto the person. This allows us to accuse that individual of what we deny in ourselves and defend ourselves from painful thoughts and feelings. But when we project, we also escalate our conflicts with others, become suspicious, and fail to see the people in our lives accurately. A second (and more difficult) type of projection is an unmet need we have pushed into shadow. We project our unmet needs onto people who do the things that we ourselves are afraid to do. Here are four steps for defusing a shadow projection.

Step 1: Pay Attention to Intense Feelings

Pay attention when someone sets you off without actually doing anything on purpose to you. Ask yourself: Did this person actually cross a line? Was there an actual transgression against me, or am I taking this person's personality personally? Authentic anger requires a transgression, a lie, a betrayal, and an insult. Shadow projection is anger without transgression. You know you're projecting when you're ranting to yourself about someone who isn't intentionally bothering you. The same goes for an unmet need. When you're set off by someone who is "getting away with something," you may be triggered. You can tell you're projecting an unmet need when you feel both disapproval and envy at the same time. Pay attention if you catch yourself thinking things like, "I wish I could shoot my mouth off like so and so and say whatever I want, but I have manners." You may be articulating an unmet need in your shadow.

Step 2: Name It and Claim It

Upon realizing that you're projecting your shadow, the next step is to identify what part of your shadow you're projecting. Are you projecting your own arrogance or pettiness onto a person showing those traits? Are you projecting your bossiness or know-it-all onto a controlling or boorish person? Are you projecting an unmet need onto a straight-talking person, a person willing to break rules, or a person who knows how to relax? Like any shadow, identifying it and putting it in context with the past defuses its energy.

Step 3: Call Out Your Projection

Call out and own your projection: "Yes, my co-worker is being totally arrogant again and I'm projecting my arrogance because sometimes I do the exact same thing." "Yes, there's my mom micro-managing everyone—just like I do when I'm freaked out." "There's my neighbor, going out without any makeup, and it pisses me off because I wish I was that confident." "I can't believe my co-worker bragged to the boss! It gets me because I wish I could talk up my accomplishments without feeling self-conscious." "My sister is so rude sometimes, but I wish I could speak my mind like that."

Step 4: Choose Your Emotion

Shadow projection is based on fear—fear of seeing a scary or shameful part of ourselves. We need to pick a different emotion so our responses will follow. For a straight-up projection, we may need a simple moment of humility. We need to see when someone else's bad behavior echoes our own by admitting to our moments of greed, pettiness, or fear. When we do this, we see both ourselves and others more accurately. We may need a moment of acceptance regarding an unmet need. We may need to speak our mind or say what we want more often. We may need to start saying "no" more often or to trust another more with our vulnerability. The more we find a functional and healthy way to meet an unmet need, the less we will project them onto others. In this next section, I will discuss how to defuse the types of shadows we have around confrontation itself. In this way, we prepare ourselves emotionally before facing a challenging situation or person.

CONFRONTING THE SHADOWS OF CONFRONTATION

When it comes to confrontation, most of us have either a fear shadow or an anger shadow that follows our conditioning as children and our primitive flight or fight response. The problem is that we often drag emotions from childhood that handicap our ability to be skillful before we have even begun to confront someone else. Many of us have a fear shadow around confrontation. As children, we learned to accommodate and defer to the wishes or aggression of others in order to feel safe. We grew up in fear of hurting others or being hurt ourselves and learned to be conflict avoidant. This can lead to an avoidant or accommodating confrontation style where we either avoid giving information in full or advice in such a way that it is easy for others to dismiss.

Some of us have an anger shadow over being challenged or corrected. We confuse being misinformed with being ashamed and take it too personally when someone does not agree with our point of view or suggestions. As children, we learned that we had to fight to get what we needed or to be heard and now bring that same aggression into the present. We see disagreement as a personal attack of our own experience, knowledge, skill, and competency. This can lead to a very competitive style that alienates others and sabotages our efforts to influence them. Remember also that others act out of *their* shadow. Another person's aggressive response to our advice may have much more to do with their own personal shadows than anything we are actually saying or doing. When someone is projecting on you, remember that individual is afraid of something and try not to take it personally.

Setting Goals for a Confrontation

It is also important to decide what we want from a confrontation before we engage. Different goals entail different levels of commitment and skill from us. For example, a basic goal may be to simply present information or advice to someone. In this instance, we are looking to inform more than influence. If we are hoping to influence someone in the long run, a good first step is to inform them. A more complex goal is to motivate someone to act on our information or advice. In this case, we are working to influence someone's behavior which takes more work, skill, and interaction with them. Finally, we may be seeking to hold another person accountable in order to see an improvement in their behavior or performance. This is the biggest challenge because it involves calling the person out, describing the gap between what they are doing and what needs to happen, and then showing them a way forward.

SUPPORTIVE CONFRONTATION MESSAGES: SPEAKING SKILLFULLY IN TENSE SITUATIONS

Within both chapter 3 and this chapter, we have seen a number of Supportive Confrontation messages employed to discuss and correct biases and biased behavior. In this section, I will provide some theoretical background and then break these message strategies down into their components. There are a number of communication perspectives that inform the structure and strategy of supportive confrontation messages. These perspectives include Burleson and Goldsmith's (2004) concept of person-centered social support; MacGeorge and Hall's (2014) research on advising; and Patterson, Grenny, McMillan, and Switzler's (2013) concept of confrontation with safety. All these perspectives share a focus on providing various forms of support while attempting to influence another person's emotional state or behavior. For example, person-centered comforting entails validating the upset person's feelings and providing ego support to his or her self-image before we attempt to give advice or our perspective on how to handle such troubles. Skillful advice involves putting choices into our advising, supporting our target person's self-image, recognizing and validating any difficulty our target is having with the situation, and then offering solutions to help that individual. Confrontation with safety also involves supporting the target person's emotions and self-image and working toward collaboration in which both individuals pool their needs and goals toward a common goal.

As we have seen through our examples, Supportive Confrontation message strategies are designed to defuse the other person's defensive emotions by supporting his or her self-image and by validating his or her feelings. We are working to support the person while critiquing his or her ideas or actions. While discussing the issue, it is important to speak toward mutuality or mutual purpose. In other words, we need to emphasize the mutual goals that we share with the other person. We want that person to see that despite our perceived differences, we both want the same thing. Finally, we need to invite the other individual to collaborate actions and solutions (Patterson et al., 2013). The following offers a further description.

Defusing Defensive Emotions

Supporting the person we are critiquing is critical to effective confrontation. Patterson et al. (2013) offer a three-step strategy they term *contrasting*. Step 1 is anticipating how our target person might erroneously take offense when presented with advice or ideas that are contrary to his or her beliefs or self-image. Second, we describe the possible offense and assure the target person this is not what we intend or mean. Third, we explain exactly what we *do* mean. It is also important to support the target person's feelings and self-image as you describe the situation at hand and the role he or she plays in it (Burleson & Goldsmith, 1997). Let the person know that you understand the challenge or struggle he or she is facing (Goldsmith, 2004; MacGeorge et al., 2016). Describe some of the positive traits you see in this individual and how these traits are related to your objective (Mortenson, 2017). Finally, treat your target person's responses and challenges to you with respect and understanding even as you work to overcome these challenges.

Speak toward Mutual Purpose

What is it that you and your target person both value? What do you both want out of this situation? When it comes to dealing with bias, you may both want as fair and unbiased a workplace as possible. You might both want to operate as people of moral and ethical integrity.

Speaking toward mutual purpose helps keep the discussion focused on what benefits your target person. One strategy here is to link your objectives to your target person's pre-existing values. Show the target person how your objectives help him or her to accomplish what he or she wants as well (Patterson et al., 2013). It is also important to describe the situation without inducing blame or fear. Respectfully state the problem and how it is related to a specific mutual purpose (Senge, 1990). Use personal narratives and accounts of your success as evidence to take your advice. Personalized narratives increase perceptions of an advisor's credibility and similarity with the recipient (Wang et al., 2008).

Invite the Target into Collaboration

Attempting to influence another person is inherently threatening because we are limiting his or her freedom by telling that individual how to feel or behave. To counter this threat, we have to put choices into our advice or directives (MacGeorge et al., 2016). Such messages re-inscribe personal control and efficacy into a recipient's responses (Albrecht & Goldsmith, 2003).

As we finish our description of the problem, we should invite our target person to participate in the solution. Doing so injects a sense of choice into the intervention and invites further collaboration.

Here is another scenario following a diversity training at a workplace. While the training helped Justin to see how things needed to change, his colleague Don was angry and resistant to the concepts. As you will see, Justin's responses followed many of the supportive confrontation strategies and effectively countered some of Don's biased and defensive statements.

Don: You know what I don't understand? Here we are having this meeting about diversity and all that, and Andre didn't say anything. I mean, he's the only black guy in the room and he didn't speak up at all.
Justin: Well, I don't think it's Andre's job to teach us about racism; we have to read up and educate ourselves about it.
Don: Yeah, but don't you think he'd want to? I mean, here's his chance to give the Black man's perspective, right?
Justin: Okay, but that's like saying that you or I could give the white man's perspective—like somehow one of us could speak for all of us, and that all white dudes see things the same way. I mean, that would be pretty weird.
Don: I dunno man, I treat everyone by how they act, you know? I don't see color; I judge people on how they act, not what they look like.
Justin: I don't think it's that simple. I read that most of our racism is unconscious; we don't even know we're being racist most of time.

Don: What are you talking about? Unconscious racism, what does that even mean? Are you saying I'm racist? I've been fair with everyone I've ever met! That's what I mean—now suddenly everyone's racist no matter what we do. What a bunch of crap!

Justin: Look Don, I *know* you treat people fairly and everyone here knows you're a good guy with good intent. I agree; it's *really hard* to hear some of this stuff. It's hard for me to hear it too. But racism's more complicated than knowing that you're unfair or mean to black people. So, check this out: I read this study where these researchers sent emails to all these college professors, almost 400 of them. They were supposed to look like a student was emailing them, and the emails all said the same thing: you know, *I'm really interested in your research and want to talk to you, can I meet with you and discuss it more*—that kind of thing. The only thing they changed were the student's names on the emails. They used white names, like Chad and Stacey, and then Latinx names and Black names and Asian names. The white male names were the ones that the professors called back much more than the other ones. And these are like college professors: they're supposed to be more educated than anyone.

Don: and more liberal . . .

Justin: Right? And yet they were being unfair and racist about choosing which students to call back. I bet they had no idea they were doing that. But check this out; this is what really blew my mind. Even the Black or Latino or Asian professors picked the white male names most often.

Don: What? They didn't go with students of their own race?

Justin: No, they didn't, and it didn't matter if they were men or women either. The women professors picked the white male names more often too! See what I mean? All these people saw themselves as fair and educated and non-biased and all that—but they weren't. Again, I know you value fairness and integrity, and I do too. So I want to know about this stuff.

Don: Okay, I admit that professor study is pretty messed up. But still, how are you supposed to fix something that's unconscious?

Justin: Actually, there are lots of ways to become more conscious about this stuff. There are tests you can take that show you your biases and all kinds of research that show how unconscious bias makes it harder for black people to get jobs and get promoted. I can send you some stuff if you want. I know, you're a stand-up guy, so I figure you'd want to know about this.

Don: All right, sure. Send me that article about the professors; that was pretty crazy.

As we can see, Don fell into some common traps related to racism. First, Don tokenized one of his colleagues (Andre) by expecting him (as the only person of color in the group) to educate everyone else. Tokenism (Kanter, 1977) occurs when less than 15% of an overall work group is perceived as to be different than the rest of the group. When this happens, the "tokens" of a work group are assimilated into roles determined by the "dominates" of the group and often miss out on advancement opportunities that don't "fit" their prescribed roles. Tokens also have high visibility in their work groups and often feel like they have to work twice as hard as their peers or have to prove themselves to other group members. Finally, members of the dominant group often exaggerate the differences between them and token members within a group. Dominants in work groups may rely on tokenized colleagues from targeted racial and sexual groups to educate others in the group. Doing so not only insinuates that everyone from the targeted group is the same, it puts even greater pressure and strain on the tokenized members of the group (Byers et al., 2020; Sue et al., 2009).

Don also fell into the trap of claiming he was "color blind" when it came to race. As an ideology, color blindness proposes that racial categories do not matter and should not be considered when making decisions such as hiring or promoting people. The basic tenet of the color-blind approach is that social categories should be dismantled and disregarded, and everyone should be treated as an individual (Firebaugh & Davis, 1998; Sniderman & Piazza, 1993). Far from mitigating racial bias, the ideology of color blindness exacerbates and worsens racial attitudes, increases implicit bias, and further serves to exculpate biased people from any responsibility for their behavior and the damage it does (Richeson & Nussbaum, 2004).

Justin also references a compelling study on the effects of implicit bias among university professors in the United States by Katherine Milkman and her colleagues. After identifying the top 230 graduate programs in *U.S. News and World Report*, Milkman and her colleagues sent fictional emails to a sample of over 6,500 graduate professors. They balanced out the number of white male professors in the study with equal number of women professors and professors of color. These emails all said the same thing: they were from graduate students who were really interested in the professor's research and they would like to meet the professor in a week's time.

The only difference was the name of the fictional student. These varied by gender and/or ethnicity which included white American, black American, Indian, Latinx, and Chinese male and female names. The researchers found that professors agreed to meet the students with white male names 26% more often than students with female or ethnic names. Moreover, female professors and professors of color granted more personal access to students with white male names than other students. In other words, researchers saw no "matching bias" (i.e., a Chinese female professor choosing to respond to a Chinese female student instead of white male student). In other words, the professors also showed bias against students of their own gender and ethnic group (Milkman, Akinola, & Chugh, 2012).

SUPPORTIVE CONFRONTATION STRATEGIES

Nothing triggers a person's shadow like confrontation. The real trick is to support the person while critiquing his or her behavior. Here are some strategies.

Know Your Shadow Around Confrontation

Confrontation is either fight or flight, and our shadows respond the same way. If you have a fear or guilt shadow around confrontation, you may be too accommodating to stand your ground and you might cave in. Remember that authentic guilt requires an agreement that you've broken. If you've made no agreement, then feeling guilty is a waste of time. If you have an anger shadow (or a shadow around "being wrong"), you may come off as too aggressive and escalate hostilities if you don't get your way. Remember that authentic anger requires a transgression; someone must have crossed a line with you. Anger without a transgression is just indulging aggression, and that's counterproductive.

Identify Your Confrontation Shadow

If confrontation produces fear, remind yourself the fear is from childhood and that you have the skills to be supportive and prevent things from escalating. If confrontation produces aggression, remind yourself that being effective is more than just being right. You don't need to get mad; you need to stay skillful and that means staying supportive.

Choose Your Objective for the Confrontation

Do you want to inform the person, motivate that individual to act, or to change his or her behavior? Is your goal to motivate this individual to improve his or her attitude or performance, or perhaps to hold him or her accountable for a failed expectation? Informing someone is easier than motivating them, so you may have to start out modestly if this is an initial confrontation. Holding another person accountable involves hearing his or her point of view and diagnosing the underlying problem behind the lapse: Is it a matter of ability, motivation, and information?

Be Supportive and Speak Toward Mutuality

Anticipate how the other person may be mistakenly offended or upset by your message. Reassure him or her that this is not what you mean, and then explain exactly what you do mean. Describe the issue at hand and what you believe needs to happen, while speaking toward mutuality. Emphasize the goals, values, and common purpose that you share with the other person while avoiding any kind of blame. Focus on the other person's good intentions and efforts. Keep tying your description of the problem to a specific mutual purpose you both share. Close with a question that invites the other person to participate in a solution.

AN EXPLORATORY QUALITATIVE ANALYSIS OF SUPPORTIVE CONFRONTATION STRATEGIES

At this point, we have portrayed supportive confrontation strategies in hypothetical situations to illustrate the difference between skillful and unskillful confrontations. In this next section, we will explore the efficacy of supportive confrontation strategies in actual confrontations by utilizing a qualitative analysis conducted for this chapter.

After securing IRB approval and gaining consent from participants, I collected 21 supportive confrontation reports written by students who underwent the intervention as part of a cocurricular leadership program on my campus. For this intervention, students participated in five virtual seminars via Zoom. As part of the intervention, students filled out and interpreted their responses to the Strengths and Shadows diagnostic questionnaire and engaged in a number of reflection and discussion exercises related to their personal shadows and the effects these factors had on their behavior. Students also wrote three reports that documented their attempts at different emotional and behavioral skills as writing assignments.

The reports I analyzed here are the third of three reports the students wrote as part of the intervention. The first report documents the students' attempts to defuse their emotions when their shadows were triggered by situations; the second documents their attempts to defuse and to own their shadow projections when they are activated by people they perceive as difficult. This third report represents the culmination of their skills and asks them to document their attempts to confront another person supportively. All of these reports are anonymous and ungraded, so students are free to write whatever they wish. The directions for the report are in figure 7.1.

Of the 21 reports, 5 described hypothetical situations and responses (what the person would do or wants to do) and were not used in the analysis. The remaining 16 reports describe actual confrontations. Two of these reports describe situations in which the writers themselves were confronted by others, and how they used supportive confrontation strategies to better take criticism from others. The remaining reports describe the writer's attempts to confront another person supportively. Of these, 12 writers report a successful outcome to the conflict and 4 writers describe an outcome that laid the groundwork for further discussions to work on the issues or behaviors. None of the writers describes any failed outcomes.

I employed a reflexive thematic analysis as described by Braun and Clarke (2006, 2013) to analyze the data. Unlike traditional qualitative methods, Braun and Clarke's reflexive thematic analysis is not bound by methodological commitments. This frees analysts to draw on the theoretical framework of their choosing to make sense of their data. Moreover, a reflexive thematic analysis is an appropriate method to examine participants' lived experiences, as well as to identify the social processes that shape experiences, meanings, and assumptions (Braun & Clarke, 2013).

I have been gathering and grading similar reports as part of my students' classwork for years in order to assess their personal transformation and growth with regard to emotional regulation and effective communication. The assignment is straightforward in structure, and students tend to follow the organization of the assignment in their responses. Given this, I am familiar with the types of themes that generally emerge from these reports.

I began conducting general coding by highlighting and labeling any relevant passages of text with a descriptive code. To explore patterns of meaning, similarly coded extracts, along with a description of each code, were then placed together in a table. I then collated related codes and discarded those that were not related to the confrontation described. All codes were then sorted into categories, which were then refined into themes.

Five major themes emerged from these reports: (1) sizing up and describing the problem, (2) choosing and describing objectives for the confrontation, (3) describing and managing personal shadows around the confrontation, (4) engaging in confrontation, and (5) the outcome of the confrontation.

Sizing Up the Situation

Writers discussed a number of different problems such as roommates failing to do apartment chores, issues related to COVID-19 safety measures, interpersonal rifts due to differences in politics and personalities, issues with team projects, and conflicts about job prospects with family members. Here are three examples that describe the situation:

1. Z and I have been good friends for a while, but we have constantly disagreed on things related to our differing political beliefs. And with how volatile the political climate has been over the last year, our relationship seemed like it could have spiraled down into a negative direction.
2. Recently, I had been struggling within my project group because I felt as if the workload placed upon me and two other group members were

far heavier than someone else. I was feeling overwhelmed with being the liaison between our community partner and our group and became frustrated when I reached out to my group for help and no one responded to me.
3. My confrontation revolved around an individual in my living environment not following through with what they would say they would do. They needed to temporarily utilize my working space for their own needs. They said that they would only need it for a week at the most. I was happy to oblige and moved to another area of the living environment. A week had passed, and my original working space was still not available.

As we can see, the writers of these reports chose to take on situations with real stakes involved rather than addressing shallow or surface-level problems. While the directions for the assignment do not specify describing the problem at hand, all the writers chose to discuss the issues.

Choosing Confrontation Objectives

One of the steps outlined in the assignment is to choose one's objectives for the confrontation, that is, to inform the target, to motivate them to act or change their behavior, or to hold the target person accountable for failed commitment. All the participants who wrote about active confrontations described engaging in this step before the confrontation. Here are three examples:

1. My objective was to inform the individual about how I felt and hopefully motivate them to improve their performance and contributions. I wanted to avoid them feeling as if I was mad at them or feel as if I had felt this way the whole year. I made plans to explain how the last couple of days have just been really bothering me and that I need help.
2. I carefully considered my objective so that my confrontation would be more about him changing for the better rather than him changing because I wanted him to.
3. We decided to talk to T in order to motivate her to talk to us and hopefully change her behavior, as well as have her tell us what she needed from us.

These representative examples all show Dillard's (1990, 2004) concept of *goals*, *plans*, and *actions* in that the writers were engaged in both problem-focused goals (resolving the issue) and relational-focused goals (preserving their relationship with the target person). One goal noticeably absent from the reports were concerns for self: none of the writers described goals related to feeling uncomfortable or nervous.

Describing and Managing Personal Shadows

All 16 of the participants who engaged in actual confrontations described how they integrated knowledge of their shadows into their approach for confronting their target person. For some writers, this involved naming specific shadows from their diagnostic test results or from discussions in one of the seminars. For others, it was descriptions of shadow-related emotions and experiences from childhood. In this example, the writer integrates his or her understanding of the shadow in order to better manage conflict avoidance:

> I know that my biggest shadow is not being accepted by my peers and I did not want to lose friends in the process of the confrontation. I had to recognize that the worst case scenarios that I was thinking about in my head probably would not even happen. Knowing that this fear is from my childhood helped me to speak up about my frustrations.

This writer describes being confronted by another person and using his or her knowledge to better handle being criticized:

> If anything, I have recognized something in myself lately through talking about strengths and shadows, in that I have an anger shadow where I respond to criticism or being told I'm wrong with hostility. I think this is probably something from my childhood, as we discussed when learning about strengths and shadows. When I was younger, I was used to being praised and told I'm right, especially in academic settings. Accepting when I am wrong is something I've been trying to work on, and I think I have become better over the past year. I saw something online recently that said "You don't get to decide if you've hurt someone." This really put things into perspective for me for both myself and how I relate to others—I now am more likely to apologize and work to do better than a version of myself even year or two ago would have.

Finally, this writer integrates knowledge of her or his shadow in order to be less critical of the target person he or she is confronting.

> First, I understood that with my Shadow of Critic I have to be aware that I might be trying to criticize K instead of understanding her. Second, I understand that this Shadow of Critic comes from my own issues with myself and how over critical I can be with myself. I will constantly overthink things and/or believe I might be not good enough or a failure. So, I got to remember that I'm not the

only one who's critical of themselves and that I need to focus on the positives and not the negatives.

As we can see from these descriptions, the writers made good use of their self-knowledge not only to manage their own defenses but to keep their target people from getting defensive as well. The emotional preparation shown in these examples paved the way for effective engagement with their target people.

Engaging in Confrontation

Armed with their emotional awareness, the writers then employed various forms of supportive confrontation message strategies and behaviors. In some cases, their strategies were employed to keep the target person from getting defensive. In the next example, the writer used the emotional strategies to keep her or himself calm during the confrontation:

> In talking to this individual, I explained that we had an agreement, and they were not living up to it. They explained that they were aware, and said they needed to continue to use the space because they were expecting for their situation at work that required for them to use the space to be over by then, but it was not. Because I anticipated that I might be angry, I was able to successfully remain calm, and upon hearing their reasoning, I thought that I should not be mad because the lack of vacating was due to a situation out of their control. They further went on to explain that they should be out within the next three days. Seeing as it was only three more days, I thought it would be unreasonable to be mad about this, so I told them thank you for explaining the situation and left it at that.

In this next example, the writer shows how he or she was able to employ supportive confrontation strategies in order to set better boundaries with an over-reliant friend. The writer here weaves his or her own strategies of constructive criticism and advice giving into a set of behaviors that addresses multiple issues about both the problem and the relationship to the target person.

The final step was talking to him and making sure I defused his defenses. I chose to confront him about this after one session where he called and asked for my help. After I helped him on the assignment, he mentioned how he felt bad for constantly pestering me at the last minute for homework help. I knew that I had to choose my words carefully; I couldn't tell him directly that it was bothering me and that I wanted him to stop. I let him know it didn't make me angry or upset that he was asking for my help, that I wanted to help him. I followed up my response by suggesting he start being more proactive in his education. I explained how his lack of care and procrastination for programming assignments was making it a little difficult to handle my own business. I let him know that I would still be able to help him, but it might be better for his future goals if he starts asking TAs and professors for help first, or even the discord server. I let him know that I believed he could improve his programming skills if he put in this extra effort to better them.

This next writer skillfully holds a roommate accountable for not doing her share of the common chores:

> I politely pointed out that at the beginning of the semester, all of the roommates had agreed to keep the common areas of our apartment clean, including the kitchen. I know she helps clean our living room, so I said that I appreciate how she helps out around the rest of the apartment. I believe that it was a lack of motivation that kept her from cleaning the kitchen, so by reminding her of our agreement, I hoped to motivate her to help out more and put her things away in the future. I tried to keep the tone neutral, and I even pointed out that I'm not perfect and I don't always put my stuff away, but that I typically make a conscious effort to clean up around the apartment when I see something that could use it.

Outcomes

Writers also discussed the outcomes of their confrontations. Of these, 12 writers reported a successful outcome to the conflict and 4 writers described an outcome that laid the groundwork for further discussions to work on the issues or behaviors. None of the writers describes any failed outcomes. The following examples give a good representation of the confrontation outcomes.

1. But needless to say, after about two hours of thoughtful discussion, we finally had understood each other's side for the first time. And even though we didn't often agree with what each of us believed, we at least knew that our political beliefs didn't matter as much as our relationship did.
2. The conversation went okay. They seemed a little defensive at first which made me feel bad but I knew that it was something that needed to be addressed. Everything isn't 100% perfect, but there have been improvements, so I am thankful for this activity.
3. The roommate who left their clothes apologized and said she simply forgot and immediately removed them from the dryer! This wouldn't be a big step for everyone, but as a people pleaser and gentle heart, it was for me. I'm going to continue taking small steps in my daily life to make sure that my own needs are met, and that I don't feel guilty about that.

Here is a full supportive confrontation report in which the writer confronts a roommate about his lack of COVID-19 safety. Here we can see the writer going through all the steps of supportive confrontation not only to discuss his or her issues with the roommate's casual attitude toward safety but to also work out a mutual plan of action for the future.

Confrontation can be one of the most difficult things to deal with. There are some people who love experiencing confrontation; personally I am the complete opposite. Confrontation is something that needs to be dealt with whether you want to or not. Luckily, I recently learned an important skill called supportive confrontation. Supportive confrontation is all about supporting the person while critiquing their behavior. This is an intricate process that is not easy but given the right steps and taken the right way it can be done. For this assignment I will be focusing on a time I used supportive confrontation to address my roommate during the pandemic.

First, it is important to lay the situation out. The pandemic has been very polarizing all over the world, with some taking it more seriously than others. I have taken it more seriously while my roommate has not. I visit my parents a lot and they are high risk, and it is really important that I do not give the virus to them. However, my roommate has not been taking it seriously and has been going out and partying during the pandemic. My roommate is my friend, and it is very hard to confront him. I have been avoiding conflict with him, but after learning about supportive confrontation I decided it was time to finally have a talk with him. Here is how I went about it. I first identified my shadow around confrontation. I know that I am way too accommodating, and I have a lot of trouble standing my ground. I know that as soon as the confrontation starts I will just be like "I understand" and just back down almost immediately. Knowing this shadow helped me understand what I was getting myself into and to make sure I avoided that specific shadow. Step two was to name and claim my confrontation shadow. I thought back to my childhood and remembered that when talking to my friends I would always be overshadowed by them and told I was wrong, and their opinions were always right. That memory made me realize why I fold so easily in confrontation and back down almost instantly. Now that I know where it comes from I can recognize that as my past and move onto my future.

Furthermore, the next two steps were just as important in this scenario. I decided when I was going to talk to my roommate, my goal was to inform him of my side of things and persuade him to be more cautious and understanding of my side of the story. This proved very helpful. I started by informing so he understood my situation and why this mattered to me. I could tell when talking about my situation that it was working, and he was understanding because he kept nodding his head in agreement. Following up with persuasion to instill that this is what I needed him to do, and I was not just telling him what is going on. Moving on to the last step was the most helpful in confronting him. I learned how to defuse defenses and support with mutual purpose. I anticipated how my roommate might take my statement and take it as me telling him how to live his life. I made sure to assure him multiple times that I am not telling him how to live his life, I am just expressing my concerns and telling him just something needed to change. I made sure to emphasize my goals of creating a safe environment for me and my parents and that we have a common purpose in keeping both of us safe. I closed with a question and asked him what he thought of the situation and if he could think of a good solution for the both of us. That last question really allowed us to collaborate and work together and we really got to a solution. This supportive confrontation skill really helped me get through a confrontation I have been dreading and helped me solve a very difficult problem in my life.

As we can see, the writers in this exploratory analysis skillfully confronted a number of issues with friends, roommates, family, and teammates, and they did so from a place of mental and emotional clarity. The emotional and cognitive preparation these writers described helped them better deploy effective messages and behaviors and pursue both relational and problem-focused goals during their interaction. It is also worth noting that the writers reporting here engaged in these confrontations during a year-long pandemic lockdown in 2020, an unprecedented time of emotional and physical hardship for people across the world. Despite such challenges, our writers had the confidence and impetus to step up to problematic issues in their lives. They employed an array of verbal behaviors that reduced their target person's defensive emotions while pursuing their goals of addressing and possibly solving the problem at hand. In doing so, they also showed us the emotional and behavioral strategies of supportive confrontation in action.

CONCLUSION

While it has never been easy to confront others about sensitive topics, the constant bombardment of disinformation and polarizing rhetoric from our media culture has made it even harder. Now, we are in conflict with family, coworkers, and neighbors over basic facts of science and medicine. Now, we seem unable to agree on the fundamental principles and practices that secure the democratic process. At the same time, the murder of George Floyd set off a historic upswelling of awareness and concern over racial bias and discrimination, and now, more people are more willing to talk about issues related to different forms of bias. More than ever, we need serious mental, emotional, and communicative skills to engage in these critical confrontations.

Bibliography

Albrecht, T. L., & Goldsmith, D. J. (2003). Social support, social networks, and health. In T. L. Thompson, A. M. Dorsey, K. I. Miller, & R. Parrott (Eds.), *Handbook of health communication* (pp. 263–284). Lawrence Erlbaum Associates Publishers.

Andrews, K. (2014). Toward a Black radical independent education: Black radicalism, independence and the supplementary school movement. *The Journal of Negro Education*, 83(1), 5–14. https://doi.org/10.7709/jnegroeducation.83.1.0005

Arndt, J., Greenberg, J., Solomon, S., Pyszczynski, T., & Simon, L. (1997). Suppression, accessibility of death-related thoughts, and cultural worldview defense: Exploring the psychodynamics of terror management. *Journal of Personality and Social Psychology*, 73(1), 5. https://doi.org/10.1037//0022-3514.73.1.5

Arudou, D. (2013). An introduction to Japanese society's attitudes toward race and skin color. In R. E. Hall (Ed.), *The melanin millennium: Skin color as 21st century international discourse* (pp. 49–69). Springer.

Averill, J. R. (2012). *Anger and aggression: An essay on emotion*. Springer Science & Business Media.

Babrow, A. S. (1992). Communication and problematic integration: Understanding diverging probability and value, ambiguity, ambivalence, and impossibility. *Communication Theory*, 2, 95–130.

Babrow, A. S. (1995). Communication and problematic integration: Milan Kundera's "lost letters" in the book of Laughter and forgetting. *Communication Monographs*, 62, 283–300.

Babrow, A. S. (2001). Uncertainty, value, communication, and problematic integration. *Journal of Communication*, 51, 553–571.

Babrow, A. S. (2007). Problematic integration theory. In B. B. Whaley & W. Samter (Eds.), *Explaining communication: Contemporary theories and exemplars* (pp. 2–40). Hillsdale, NJ: Lawrence Erlbaum.

Bales, R. F. (1970). *Personality and interpersonal behavior*. Hold, Rinehart & Winston.

Bales, R. F. (1999). *Social interaction systems: Theory and measurement.* New Brunsswick.
Banaji, M. R., & Greenwald, A. G. (2013). *Blindspot: Hidden biases of good people.* Bantam.
Barbee, A. P., Lawrence T., & Cunningham, M. R. (1998). When a friend is in need: Feelings about seeking, giving, and receiving social support. In P. A. Andersen & L. K. Guerrero (Eds.), *Communication and emotion: Theory, research, and applications* (pp. 369–411). Academic Press.
Bargh, J. A. (2006). What have we been priming all these years? On the development, mechanisms, and ecology of nonconscious social behavior. *European Journal Social Psychology,* 36, 147–168.
Bargh, J. A., & Chartrand, T. L. (1999). The unbearable automaticity of being. *American Psychologist,* 54, 462–479.
Bargh, J. A., Golwitzer, P. M., Lee-Chai, A., Barndollar, K., & Trotschel R. (2001). The automated will: Nonconscious activation and pursuit of behavioral goals. *Journal of Personality and Social Psychology,* 81, 1014–1027.
Barrett, L. F., Adolphs, R., Marsella, S., Martinez, A. M., & Pollak, S. D. (2019). Emotional expressions reconsidered: Challenges to inferring emotion from human facial movements. *Psychological Science in the Public Interest,* 20(1), 1–68. https://doi.org/10.1177/1529100619832930
Baxter, L. A. (1990). Dialectical contradictions in relationship development. *Journal of Social and Personal Relationships,* 7(1), 69–88. https://doi.org/10.1177/0265407590071004
Baxter, L. A. (2010). *Voicing relationships: A dialogic perspective.* Sage. https://doi.org/10.4135/9781452230344
Berger, C. R. (1997). *Planning strategic interaction.* Mahwah, NJ: Lawrence Erlbaum.
Berkowitz, L. (1993). *Aggression: Its causes, consequences, and control.* Mcgraw-Hill Book Company.
Blair, I. V. (2002). The malleability of automatic stereotypes and prejudice. *Personality and Social Psychology Review,* 6(3), 242–261. https://doi.org/10.1207/S15327957PSPR0603_8
Bosson, J. K., Pinel, E. C., & Vandello, J. A. (2010). The emotional impact of ambivalent sexism: Forecasts versus real experiences. *Sex Roles,* 62(7), 520–531. https://doi.org/10.1007/s11199-009-9664-y
Botero, I. C., & Van Dyne, L. (2009). Employee voice behavior: Interactive effects of LMX and power distance in the United States and Colombia. *Management Communication Quarterly,* 23, 84–104. https://doi.org/10.1177/0893318909335415
Boyd, R. D., & Myers, J. G. (1988). Transformative education. *International Journal of Lifelong Education,* 7(4), 261–284. https://doi.org/10.1080/0260137880070403
Boyd, W. L., Kerchner, C. T., & Blyth, M. (2008). *The transformation of great American school districts: How big cities are reshaping public education.* Harvard Education Press.
Braun, V., & Clarke, V. (2006). Using thematic analysis in psychology. *Qualitative Research in Psychology,* 3(2), 77–101. https://doi.org/10.1191/1478088706qp063oa

Braun, V., & Clarke, V. (2013). *Successful qualitative research: A practical guide for beginners.* Sage.
Brown, P., & Levinson, S. C. (1987). *Politeness: Some universals in language usage.* New York: Cambridge University. https://doi.org/10.1017/cbo9780511813085
Burgoon, J. K., & Langer, E. J. (2012). Language, fallacies, and mindlessness-mindfulness in social interaction. In B. R. Burleson (Ed.), *Communication Yearbook* (pp. 105–132). Routledge.
Burgoon, J. K., Berger, C. R. & Waldron, V. R. (2000). Mindful and interpersonal communication. *Journal of Social Issues*, 56, 105–128. https://doi.org/10.1111/0022-4537.00154
Burleson, B. R., & Goldsmith, D. J. (1997). How the comforting process works: Alleviating emotional distress through conversationally induced reappraisals. In Andersen, P. A., & Guerrero, L. K. (Eds.), *Handbook of communication and emotion: Research, theory, applications, and contexts* (pp. 245–280). Elsevier.
Burleson, B. R., Albrecht, T. L., & Sarason, I. G. (Eds.). (1994). *Communication of social support: Messages, interactions, relationships, and community.* Sage.
Burleson, B. R., & Mortenson, S. T. (2003). Explaining cultural differences in evaluations of emotional support behaviors: Exploring the mediating influences of value systems and interaction goals. *Communication Research*, 30, 113–146. https://doi.org/10.1177/0093650202250873
Buzzanell, P. M. (2000). The promise and practice of the new career and social contract: Illusions exposed and suggestions for reform. In P. M. Buzzanell (Ed.), *Rethinking organizational and managerial communication from feminist perspectives* (pp. 209–235). Thousand Oaks, CA: Sage. https://doi.org/10.4135/9781452225494.n9
Cai, D. A., & Wilson, S. R. (2000). Identity implications of influence goals: A cross-cultural comparison of interaction goals and facework. *Communication Studies*, 51, 307–328. https://doi.org/10.1080/10510970009388529
Canary, D. J. (2003). Managing interpersonal conflict: A model of events related to strategic choices. In J. O. Greene & B. R. Burleson (Eds.), *Handbook of communication and social interaction skills* (pp. 515–549). Lawrence Erlbaum Associates Publishers.
Castelli, L., Zogmaister, C., & Tomelleri, S. (2009). The transmission of racial attitudes within the family. *Developmental Psychology*, 45(2), 586–591. https://doi.org/10.1037/a0014619
Chen, S., & Chaiken, S. (1999). The heuristic-systematic model in its broader context. In S. Chaiken & Y. Trope (Eds.), *Dual-process theories in social psychology* (pp. 73–96). New York: Guilford.
Christopher, S., Dunnagan, T., Duncan, S., & Paul, L. (2001). Education for self-support: Evaluating outcomes using transformative learning theory. *Family Relations*, 50, 134–142. https://doi.org/10.1111/j.1741-3729.2001.00134.x
Clark, D. A. & Beck, A. T. (2010). *Cognitive therapy of anxiety disorders: Science and practice.* The Guilford Press.
Conrad, K., Dixon, T. L., & Zhang, Y. (2009). Controversial rap themes, gender portrayals and skin tone distortion: A content analysis of rap music videos. *Journal*

of *Broadcasting & Electronic Media*, 53(1), 134–156. https://doi.org/10.1080/08838150802643795

Conte, H. R., & Plutchik, R. (1993). The measurement of ego defenses in clinical research. In *The concept of defense mechanisms in contemporary psychology* (pp. 275–289). Springer.

Cooren, F., Kuhn, T., Cornelissen, J. P., & Clark, T. (2011). Communication, organizing and organization: An overview and introduction to the special issue. *Organization Studies*, 32(9), 1149–1170. https://doi.org/10.1177/0170840611410836

Courtney, B., Merriam, S., & Reeves, P. (1998). The centrality of meaning-making in Transformative learning: How HIV-positive adults make sense of their lives. *Adult Education Quarterly*, 48, 65–84. https://doi.org/10.1177/074171369804800203

Cramer, P. (1998). Coping and defense mechanisms: What's the difference? *Journal of Personality*, 66(6), 919–946. https://doi.org/10.1111/1467-6494.00037

Cramer, P. (2003). Personality change in later adulthood is predicted by defense mechanism use in early adulthood. *Journal of Research in Personality*, 37(1), 76–104. https://doi.org/10.1016/s0092-6566(02)00528-7

Cramer, P. (2006). *Protecting the self: Defense mechanisms in action*. Guilford Press.

Cramer, P. (2007). Longitudinal study of defense mechanisms: Late childhood to late adolescence. *Journal of Personality*, 75(1), 1–24. https://doi.org/10.1111/j.1467-6494.2006.00430.x

Cranton, P. (1994). *Understanding and promoting transformative learning: A guide for educators of adults*. Jossey-Bass Higher and Adult Education Series. Jossey-Bass.

Crews, T. B., Bodenhamer, J., & Weaver, T. (2010). Understanding true colors personality trait spectrums of hotel, restaurant, and tourism management students to enhance classroom instruction. *Journal of Teaching in Travel & Tourism*, 10(1), 22–41. https://doi.org/10.1080/15313220903558538

Cuddy, A. J., Fiske, S. T., & Glick, P. (2008). Warmth and competence as universal dimensions of social perception: The stereotype content model and the BIAS map. *Advances in Experimental Social Psychology*, 40, 61–149. https://doi.org/10.1016/s0065-2601(07)00002-0

Curry-Stevens, A. (2007). New forms of transformative education: Pedagogy for the privileged. *Journal of Transformative Education*, 5(1), 33–58. https://doi.org/10.1177/1541344607299394

Czopp, A. M., & Ashburn-Nardo, L. (2012). Interpersonal confrontations of prejudice. *Psychology of Prejudice: Contemporary Issues*, 175, 201. https://doi.org/10.31234/osf.io/jzxmy

Czopp, A. M., Monteith, M. J., & Mark, A. Y. (2006). Standing up for a change: Reducing bias through interpersonal confrontation. *Journal of Personality and Social Psychology*, 90(5), 784–803. https://doi.org/10.1037/0022-3514.90.5.784

Dardenne, B., Dumont, M., & Bollier, T. (2007). Insidious dangers of benevolent sexism: Consequences for women's performance. *Journal of Personality and Social Psychology*, 93(5), 764. https://doi.org/10.1037/0022-3514.93.5.764

Dasgupta, N. (2013). Implicit attitudes and beliefs adapt to situations: A decade of research on the malleability of implicit prejudice, stereotypes, and the self-concept.

Advances in Experimental Social Psychology, 47(7), 33–279. https://doi.org/10.1016/B978-0-12-407236-7.00005-X

Dass-Brailsford, P. (2007). Racial identity change among white graduate students. *Journal of Transformative Education*, 5(1), 59–78. https://doi.org/10.1177%2F1541344607299210

de Boer, A. G., van Lanschot, J. J., Stalmeier, P. F., van Sandick, J. W., Hulscher, J. B., de Haes, J. C., & Sprangers, M. A. (2004). Is a single-item visual analogue scale as valid, reliable and responsive as multi-item scales in measuring quality of life? *Quality of Life Research*, 13, 311–320. https://doi.org/10.1023/b:qure.0000018499.64574.1f

DiAngelo, R. (2018). *White fragility: Why it's so hard for white people to talk about racism*. Beacon Press.

Dillard, J. P. (1990). A goal-driven model of interpersonal influence. In J. P. Dillard (Ed.), *Seeking compliance: The production of interpersonal influence messages* (pp. 41–56). Gorsuch Scarisbrick.

Dillard, J. P. (2004). The goals-plan-action model of interposal influence. In J. S. Seiter & R. H. Gass (Eds.), *Perspectives on persuasion, social influence, and compliance gaining* (pp. 185–206). Boston: Allyn & Bacon.

Dillard, J. P., Carson, C. L., Bernard, C. J., Laxova, A., & Farrell, P. M. (2004). An analysis of communication following newborn screening for cystic fibrosis. *Health Communication*, 16(2), 197–205. https://doi.org/10.1207/S15327027HC1602_4

Dillard, J. P., Segrin, C., & Harden, J. M. (1989). Primary and secondary goals in the production of interpersonal influence message. *Communication Monographs*, 56, 19–38. https://doi.org/10.1080/03637758909390247

Dixon, A. R., & Telles, E. E. (2017). Skin color and colorism: Global research, concepts, and measurement. *Annual Review of Sociology*, 43, 405–424. https://doi.org/10.1146/annurev-soc-060116-053315

Doucet, F., & Adair, J. K. (2013). Addressing race and inequity in the classroom. *Young Children*, 68(5), 88. https://doi.org/10.1177/074171369804801199-X***

Dovidio, J. F., & Gaertner, S. L. (1986). *Prejudice, discrimination, and racism*. Academic Press.

Dovidio, J. F., Kawakami, K., Johnson, C., Johnson, B., & Howard, A. (1997). On the nature of prejudice: Automatic and controlled processes. *Journal of Experimental Social Psychology*, 33(5), 510–540. https://doi.org/10.1006/jesp.1997.1331

Eagly, A. H., & Karau, S. J. (2002). Role congruity theory of prejudice toward female leaders. *Psychological Bulletin*, 109, 573–598. https://doi.org/10.1037/0033-295x.109.3.573

Esposito, L., & Romano, V. (2014). Benevolent racism: Upholding racial inequality in the name of Black empowerment. *Western Journal of Black Studies*, 38(2), 69–83. https://doi.org/10.1177/0093650208326460

Fairhurst, G. (2009). Considering context in discursive leadership research. *Human Relations*, 62, 1607–1633. https://doi.org/10.1177/0018726709346379

Fairhurst, G. T. (2007). *Discursive leadership: In conversation with leadership psychology*. Sage. https://doi.org/10.2189/asqu.2009.54.1.162

Falbe, C. M., & Yukl, G. (1992). Consequences for managers of using single influence tactics and combinations of tactics. *Academy of Management Journal*, 35, 638–652. https://doi.org/10.5465/256490

Fazio, R. H. (2007). Attitudes as object–evaluation associations of varying strength. *Social Cognition*, 25, 603–637. https://doi.org/10.1521/soco.2007.25.5.603

Fazio, R. H., & Hilden, L. E. (2001). Emotional reactions to a seemingly prejudiced response: The role of automatically activated racial attitudes and motivation to control prejudiced reactions. *Personality and Social Psychology Bulletin*, 27(5), 538–549. https://doi.org/10.1177/0146167201275003

Fazio, R. H., Jackson, J. R., Dunton, B. C., & Williams, C. J. (1995). Variability in automatic activation as an unobtrusive measure of racial attitudes: A bona fide pipeline? *Journal of Personality and Social Psychology*, 69(6), 1013–1027. https://doi.org/10.1037/0022-3514.69.6.1013

Fiske, S. T., & Taylor, S. E. (2013). *Social cognition: From brains to culture*. Sage.

Fiske, S. T., & Taylor, S. E. (1991). *Social cognition*. Mcgraw-Hill.

Fiske, S. T., Cuddy, A. J., Glick, P., & Xu, J. (2002). A model of (often mixed) stereotype content: Competence and warmth respectively follow from perceived status and competition. *Journal of Personality and Social Psychology*, 82(6), 878. https://doi.org/10.1037/0022-3514.82.6.878

Flores, R., & Telles, E. (2012). Social stratification in Mexico: Disentangling color, ethnicity, and class. *American Sociological Review*, 77(3), 486–494. https://doi.org/10.1177%2F0003122412444720

Folger, J. P., Hewes, D. E., & Poole, M. S. (1984). Coding social interaction. In B. Dervin & M. Voight (Eds.), *Progress in communication sciences* (Vol. 4, pp. 115–161). Ablex.

Galinsky, A. D., Ku, G., & Wang, C. S. (2005). Perspective-taking and self-other overlap: Fostering social bonds and facilitating social coordination. *Group Processes & Intergroup Relations*, 8(2), 109–124. https://doi.org/10.1177/1368430205051060

Gardner, D. G., Cummings, L. L., Dunham, R. B., & Pierce, J. L. (1998). Single-item versus multiple-item measurement scales: An empirical comparison. *Educational and Psychological Measurement*, 58(6), 898–915. https://doi.org/10.1177/0013164498058006003

Gigerenzer, G. (2000). *Adaptive thinking: Rationality in the real word*. Oxford University Press.

Girod, S., Fassiotto, M., Grewal, D., Ku, M. C., Sriram, N., Nosek, B. A., & Valantine, H. (2016). Reducing implicit gender leadership bias in academic medicine with an educational intervention. *Academic Medicine*, 91, 1143–1150. https://doi.org/10.1097/acm.0000000000001099

Glick, P., & Fiske, S. T. (1996). The ambivalent sexism inventory: Differentiating hostile and benevolent sexism. *Journal of Personality and Social Psychology*, 70(3), 491. https://doi.org/10.1037/0022-3514.70.3.491

Glick, P., & Fiske, S. T. (2001). An ambivalent alliance: Hostile and benevolent sexism as complementary justifications for gender inequality. *American Psychologist*, 56(2), 109. https://doi.org/10.1037/0003-066X.56.2.109

Goldberg, L. R. (1990). An alternative "description of personality": The big-five factor structure. *Journal of Personality and Social Psychology*, 59(6), 1216. https://doi.org/10.1037/0022-3514.59.6.1216

Goldsmith, D. J. (2004). *Communicating social support.* Cambridge University Press.

Good, J. J., & Rudman, L. A. (2010). When female applicants meet sexist interviewers: The costs of being a target of benevolent sexism. *Sex Roles*, 62(7), 481–493. link.springer.com/article/10.1007/s11199-009-9685-6

Gottman, J. M. (1994). An agenda for marital therapy. In S. M. Johnson & L. S. Greenberg (Eds.), *The heart of the matter: Perspectives on emotion in marital: Perspectives on emotion in marital therapy* (pp. 256–293). Routledge.

Grabov, V. (1997). The many facets of transformative learning theory and practice. In P. Cranton (Ed.), *Transformative learning in action: Insights from practice* (pp. 89–96). Jossey-Bass.

Greene, J. O. (1997). A second generation action assembly theory. In J. O. Greene (Ed.), *Message production: Advances in communication theory* (pp. 151–170). Mahwah, NJ: Lawrence Erlbaum.

Greenwald, A. G., & Banaji, M. R. (2017). The implicit revolution: Reconceiving the relation between conscious and unconscious. *American Psychologist*, 72(9), 861–871. https://doi.org/10.1037/amp0000238

Greenwald, A. G., & Krieger, L. H. (2006). Implicit bias: Scientific foundations. *California Law Review*, 94(4), 945–967. https://doi.org/10.2307/20439056

Hale, C. A., & Fleiss, J. L. (1993). Interval estimation under two study designs for kappa with binary classifications. *Biometrics*, 49, 523–534.

Hample, D. (2018). *Interpersonal arguing.* Peter Lang. https://doi.org/10.3726/b12877

Hare, P. A. (2000). Social interaction systems: Theory and measurement: Book review. *Group Dynamics: Theory, Research, and Practice* 4(1), 199–208.

Heckhausen, H., & Gollwitzer, P. M. (1985). Thought contents and cognitive functioning in motivational versus volitional states of mind. *Motivation and Emotion*, 11, 101–120.

Hill, C. (March 29, 2016). Implicit bias and AAUW implicit association test on gender and leadership [PDF]. Retrieved from https://www.aauw.org/resource/iat/

Hochschild, J. L., & Weaver, V. (2007). The skin color paradox and the American racial order. *Social Forces*, 86(2), 643–670. https://doi.org/10.1093/sf/86.2.643

Hoffman, M. L. (2013). Development of prosocial motivation: Empathy and guilt. In H. Beilin (Ed.), *The development of prosocial behavior* (pp. 281–313). Academic Press.

Hogg, M. A., & Terry, D. J. (2000). Social identity and self-categorization processes in organizational contexts. *Academy of Management Review*, 25, 121–140. https://doi.org/10.2307/259266

Hollis, J. (2008). *Why good people do bad things: Understanding our darker selves.* Penguin Books.

Hughes, M., & Hertel, B. R. (1990). The significance of color remains: A study of life chances, mate selection, and ethnic consciousness among Black Americans. *Social Forces*, 68(4), 1105–1120. https://doi.org/10.1093/sf/68.4.1105

Hunter, M. (2007). The persistent problem of colorism: Skin tone, status, and inequality. *Sociology Compass*, 1(1), 237–254. https://doi.org/10.1111/j.1751-9020.2007.00006.x

Hunter, M. L. (2011). Buying racial capital: Skin-bleaching and cosmetic surgery in a globalized world. *The Journal of Pan African Studies*, 4(4), 142–164. https://www.jpanafrican.org/docs/vol4no4/HUNTER%20Final.pdf

Hyers, L. L. (2007). Resisting prejudice every day: Exploring women's assertive responses to anti-Black racism, anti-Semitism, heterosexism, and sexism. *Sex Roles*, 56(1), 1–12.

Insko, C. A., & Schopler, J. (1967). Triadic consistency: A statement of affective-cognitive-conative consistency. *Psychological Review*, 74, 361. https://doi.org/10.1037/h0020278

Isaac, C., Lee, B., & Carnes, M. (2009). Interventions that affect gender bias in hiring: A systematic review. *Academic Medicine: Journal of the Association of American Medical Colleges*, 84, 1440. https://doi.org/10.1097/acm.0b013e3181b6ba00

Jablonski, N. G. (2012). *Living color: The biological and social meaning of skin color*. Berkeley: University of California Press

Johnson, B. T., & Eagly, A. H. (1989). Effects of involvement on persuasion: A meta-analysis. *Psychological Bulletin*, 106, 290–314. https://doi.org/10.1037/0033-2909.106.2.290

Johnson, R. A. (1993). *Owning your own shadow: Understanding the dark side of the psyche*. Harper.

Johnson, S. K., Murphy, S. E., Zewdie, S., & Reichard, R. J. (2008). The strong sensitive type: Effects of gender stereotypes and leadership prototypes on the evaluation of female and female leaders. *Organizational Behavior and Human Decision Processes*, 106, 39–60. https://doi.org/10.1016/j.obhdp.2007.12.002

Jost, J. T., & Kay, A. C. (2005). Exposure to benevolent sexism and complementary gender stereotypes: Consequences for specific and diffuse forms of system justification. *Journal of Personality and Social Psychology*, 88(3), 498. psycnet.apa.org/buy/2005-01818-006

Jung, C. G. (1969). *The structure and dynamics of the psyche (RFC Hull, Trans.)*. The collected works of CG Jung, 8.

Jung, C. G., Campbell, J., & Hull, R. F. C. (1971). *The portable jung* (p. 659). Penguin Books.

Kahneman, D. (2011). *Thinking, fast and slow*. Macmillan.

Kang, J. (2012). Communications law: Bits of bias. In J. D. Levinson & R. J. Smith (Eds.), *Implicit racial bias across the law* (pp. 132–145). Cambridge University Press.

Keith, V. M., & Herring, C. (1991). Skin tone and stratification in the Black community. *American Journal of Sociology*, 97(3), 760–778. https://doi.org/10.1086/229819

Kerssen-Griep, J., & Eifler, K. (2008). White novice teachers learn alongside their African American high school mentees. *Journal of Transformative Education*, 6(4), 251–269. https://doi.org/10.1177/1541344608330125

Klaczynski, P. A. (2001). Framing effects on adolescent task representations, analytic and heuristic processing, and decision making implications for the normative/descriptive gap. *Applied Developmental Psychology*, 22, 289–309.

Knight, A. (2010). Racism, revolution, and indigenismo: Mexico, 1910–1940. In R. Graham (Ed.), *The idea of race in Latin America, 1870–1940* (pp. 71–113). University of Texas Press.

Koenig, A. M., Eagly, A. H., Mitchell, A. A., & Ristikari, T. (2011). Are leader stereotypes masculine? A meta-analysis of three research paradigms. *Psychological Bulletin*, 137, 616–642. https://doi.org/10.1037/a0023557

Langer, E. J. (1989). *Mindfulness*. Addison-Wesley.

Lazarus, R. S., & Lazarus, B. N. (1994). *Passion and reason: Making sense of our emotions*. Oxford University Press.

Leonardo, Z. (2004). The color of supremacy: Beyond the discourse of 'white privilege'. *Educational Philosophy and Theory*, 36(2), 137–152. https://doi.org/10.1111/j.1469-5812.2004.00057.x

Lewis, K. M., Harris, S., Camp, C., Kalala, W., Jones, W., Ellick, K. L., & Younge, S. (2013). The historical and cultural influences of skin bleaching in Tanzania. In R. E. Hall (Ed.), *The melanin millennium* (pp. 19–38). Springer Science & Business Media.

Lim, T. S., & Bowers, J. W. (1991). Facework solidarity, approbation, and tact. *Human Communication Research*, 17, 415–450. https://doi.org/10.1111/j.1468-2958.1991.tb00239.x

Lupton, D. (1992). Discourse analysis: A new methodology for understanding the ideologies of health and illness. *Australian Journal of Public Health*, 16(2), 145–150.

MacGeorge, E. L., & Hall, E. D. (2014). Relationship advice. In C. R. Agnew (Ed.), *Social influences on romantic relationships: Beyond the dyad* (pp. 188–208). Cambridge University Press. https://doi.org/10.1017/CBO9781139333610.012

MacGeorge, E. L., Guntzviller, L. M., Hanasono, L. K., & Feng, B. (2016). Testing advice response theory in interactions with friends. *Communication Research*, 43(2), 211–231. https://doi.org/10.1177/0093650213510938

Maxwell, M. L., Abrams, J. A., & Belgrave, F. Z. (2016). Redbones and earth mothers: The influence of rap music on African American girls' perceptions of skin color. *Psychology of Music*, 44(6), 1488–1499. https://doi.org/10.1177/0305735616643175

McIntosh, P. (2004). White privilege: Unpacking the invisible knapsack. In P. S. Rothenberg (Ed.), *Race, class, and gender in the United States: An integrated study* (pp. 188–192). Macmillan.

Mezirow, J. (1991). *Transformative dimensions of adult learning*. Jossey-Bass.

Mezirow, J. (1994). Understanding transformation theory. *Adult Education Quarterly*, 44(4), 222–232. https://doi.org/10.1037/0022-3514.69.6.1013

Mezirow, J. (1997). Transformative learning: Theory to practice. *New Directions For Adult And Continuing Education*, 1997(74), 5–12.

Mezirow, J. (1998). On critical reflection. *Adult Education Quarterly*, 48(3), 185–198.

Mezirow, J., & Taylor, E. W. (Eds.). (2009). *Transformative learning in practice: Insights from community, workplace, and higher education*. John Wiley & Sons.

Middleton, V. A., Anderson, S. K., & Banning, J. H. (2009). The journey to understanding privilege: A meta-narrative approach. *Journal of Transformative Education*, 7(4), 294–311. https://doi.org/10.1177/1541344610386868

Mo, C. H. (2015). The consequences of explicit and implicit gender attitudes and candidate quality in the calculations of voters. *Political Behavior*, 37, 357–395. https://doi.org/10.1007/s11109-014-9274-4

Monk Jr, E. P. (2014). Skin tone stratification among black Americans, 2001–2003. *Social Forces*, 92(4), 1313–1337. https://doi.org/10.1093/sf/sou007

Moore, R., & Gillette, D. (1991). *Rediscovering the mature archetypes of the mature masculine*. Harper Collins.

Mortenson, S. (2007). Raising the question #7 should we teach personal transformation as a part of interpersonal communication? If so, how is it done?. *Communication Education*, 56(3), 401–408. https://doi.org/10.1080/03634520701349198

Mortenson, S. (2009). Interpersonal trust and social skill in seeking social support among Chinese and Americans. *Communication Research*, 36(1), 32–53. https://doi.org/10.1177/0093650208326460

Mortenson, S. (2017). Confronting implicit and benevolent bias in teams. In C. M. Cunningham, H. M. Crandall, & A. M. Dare (Eds.), *Gender, communication, and the leadership gap* (pp. 47–68). Information Age Publishing. https://doi.org/10.1080/00497878.2019.1580525

Mortenson, S., Creasy, M., & Geyer, C. (2020). *The influence of interpersonal projection on attributes of negative conflict among college roommates*. Paper presented at the Eastern Communication Association Conference, Baltimore, MA.

Mortenson, S., Liu, M., Burleson, B. R., & Liu, Y. (2006). A fluency of feeling: Exploring cultural and individual differences (and similarities) related to skilled emotional support. *Journal of Cross-Cultural Psychology*, 37(4), 366–385. https://doi.org/10.1177/0022022106288475

Mortenson, S., Luchey S., & Creasy M. (2015). *When the rubber hits the road: Tools and challenges for student leaders*. Invited Presentation at the Association of Leadership Educators Conference, Washington D.C.

Moskowitz, G. B., Skurnik, I., & Galinsky, A. D. (1999). The history of dual-process notions, and the future of preconscious control. In S. Chaiken & Y. Trope (Eds.), *Dual-process theories in social psychology* (pp. 12–36). The Guilford Press.

Mumby, D. K., & Stohl, C. (1991). Power and discourse in organization studies: Absence and the dialectic of control. *Discourse & Society*, 2, 313–332. https://doi.org/10.1177/0957926591002003004

Myers, I. B., & McCaulley, M. H. (1988). *Myers-Briggs type indicator: MBTI*. Palo Alto: Consulting Psychologists Press.

Nagy, M. S. (2002). Using a single-item approach to measure facet job satisfaction. *Journal of Occupational and Organizational Psychology*, 75, 77–86. https://doi.org/10.1348/096317902167658

Norwood, C. (2013). Perspective in Africana feminism; exploring expressions of Black feminism/womanism in the African diaspora. *Sociology Compass*, 7(3), 225–236. https://doi.org/10.1111/soc4.12025

O'Keefe, B. J. (1988). The logic of message design. *Communication Monographs*, 55, 80–103.
Ostrom, E. (1998). A behavioral approach to the rational choice theory of collective action: Presidential address, American Political Science Association, 1997. *American Political Science Review*, 1–22.
Patterson, G. R., Littman, R. A., & Bricker, W. (1967). Assertive behavior in children: A step toward a theory of aggression. *Monographs of the Society for Research in Child Development*, 32(5), iii–43. https://doi.org/10.2307/1165737
Patterson, K., Grenny, J., McMillan, R., Switzler, A., & Maxfield, D. (2013). *Crucial accountability: Tools for resolving violated expectations, broken commitments, and bad behavior*. McGraw-Hill Professional.
Pearce, W. B. (1976). The coordinated management of meaning: A rules-based theory of interpersonal communication. In G. R. Miller (Ed.), *Explorations in interpersonal communication*. Sage.
Pearce, W. B., & Cronen, V. E. (1980). *Communication, action, and meaning: The creation of social realities*. Praeger.
Pearce, W. B., & Pearce, K. A. (2000). Extending the theory of the coordinated management of meaning (CMM) through a community dialogue process. *Communication Theory*, 10(4), 405–423.
Petty, R. E., & Cacioppo, J. T. (1986). *Communication and persuasion: Central and peripheral routes to attitude change*. New York: Springer-Verlag.
Petty, R. E., Fabrigar, L. R., & Wegener, D. T. (2003). Emotional factors in attitudes and persuasion. In R. J. Davidson, K. R. Scherer, & H. H. Goldsmith (Eds.), *Series in affective science: Handbook of affective sciences* (pp. 752–772). Oxford University Press.
Petty, R. E., Harkins, S. G., & Williams, K. D. (1980). The effects of group diffusion on cognitive effort on attitudes: An information processing view. *Journal of Personality and Social Psychology*, 38, 81–92. https://doi.org/10.1037/0022-3514.38.1.81
Plutchik, R. (1995). A theory of ego defenses. In H. Conte & R. Plutchik (Eds.), *Ego defenses: Theory and measurement* (pp. 13–37). New York, NY: John Wiley & Sons.
Putnam, L. L., & Cooren, F. (2004). Alternative perspectives on the role of text and agency in constituting organizations. *Organization*, 11, 323–333. https://doi.org/10.1177/1350508404041995
Ragins, B. R., & Winkel, D. E. (2011). Gender, emotion and power in work relationships. *Human Resource Management Review*, 21(4), 377–393.
Ramasubramanian, S., & Oliver, M. B. (2007). Activating and suppressing hostile and benevolent racism: Evidence for comparative media stereotyping. *Media Psychology*, 9(3), 623–646. https://doi.org/10.1080/15213260701283244
Reskin, B. (2005). Unconsciousness raising. *Regional Review*, 14(3), 32–37. https://doi.org/10.1080/15313220903558538
Richo, D. (2008). *When the past is present: Healing the emotional wounds that sabotage our relationships*. Shambhala Publications.
Riso, D. R., & Hudson, R. (2000). *Understanding the enneagram: The practical guide to personality types*. Houghton Mifflin Harcourt.

Roets, A., Kruglanski, A. W., Kossowska, M., Pierro, A., & Hong, Y. Y. (2015). The motivated gatekeeper of our minds: New directions in need for closure theory and research. In *Advances in experimental social psychology* (Vol. 52, pp. 221–283). Academic Press.

Rutland, A., Cameron, L., Milne, A., & McGeorge, P. (2005). Social norms and self-presentation: Children's implicit and explicit intergroup attitudes. *Child Development*, 76(5), 451–466. https://doi.org/10.1111/j.1467-8624.2005.00856

Samp, J. A., & Solomon, D. H. (1998). Communicative responses to problematic events in close relationships: The variety and facets of goals. *Communication Research*, 25, 66–95. https://doi.org/10.1177/009365098025001003

Sandberg, S. (2010, December). *Why we have too few women leaders*. TED. https://www.ted.com/talks/sheryl_sandberg_why_we_have_too_few_women_leaders

Saraswati, L. A. (2013). *Seeing beauty, sensing race in transnational Indonesia*. University of Hawaii Press.

Seltzer, R., & Smith, R. C. (1991). Color differences in the Afro-American community and the differences they make. *Journal of Black Studies*, 21(3), 279–286. doi/pdf/10.1177/002193479102100303

Senge, P. M. (1990). *The fifth discipline: The art and craft of the learning organization*. Random House.

Shi, X. (2009). *From our thoughts to actual messages: An application and extension of the GPA model in explicating advice message production in an upward influence context*. Doctoral dissertation, Purdue University.

Shi, X. (2013). Cognitive responses in advice planning: An examination of thought content and its impact on message features under high vs. low effortful thinking modes. *Journal of Language and Social Psychology*, 32, 311–334. https://doi.org/10.1177/0261927X12470112

Shi, X., & Wilson, S. R. (2010). Upward influence in contemporary Chinese organizations: Explicating the effects of influence goal type and multiple goal importance on message reasoning and politeness. *Management Communication Quarterly*, 24(4), 579–606. https://doi.org/10.1177/0893318910376913

Shi, X., Brinthaupt, T. M., & McCree, M. (2015). The relationship of self-talk frequency to communication apprehension and public speaking anxiety. *Personality and Individual Differences*, 75, 125–129. https://doi.org/10.1016/j.paid.2014.11.023

Shi, X., Brinthaupt, T., & McCree, M. (2017). Understanding the influence of self-critical, self-managing, and social-assessing self-talk on performance outcomes in a public speaking context. *Imagination, Cognition and Personality*, 36(4), 356–378. https://doi.org/10.1177/0276236617708740

Shi, X., & Wilson, S. R. (2017). Influence. *The International Encyclopedia of Organizational Communication*, 1–13. https://doi.org/10.1002/9781118955567.wbieoc107

Sillars, A. L. (1981). Attributions and interpersonal conflict resolution. In E. Borgida, N. Brekke, J. H. Harvey, W. J. Ickes, & R. F. Kidd (Eds.), *New directions in attribution research*, 3 (pp. 279–305). Psychology Press.

Skagerlund, K., Forsblad, M., Slovic, P., & Västfjäll, D. (2020). The affect heuristic and risk perception–stability across elicitation methods and individual cognitive abilities. *Frontiers in Psychology*, 11, 1–10.

Sommers-Flanagan, J., & Sommers-Flanagan, R. (2018). *Counseling and psychotherapy theories in context and practice: Skills, strategies, and techniques.* John Wiley & Sons.

Staats, C. (2014). *State of the science: Implicit bias review 2014, Kirwan Institute for the Study of Race and Ethnicity.* The Ohio State University. Retrieved from http://www.kirwaninstitute.osu.edu/wp-content/uploads/2014/03/2014- implicit-bias.pdf

Staats, C., Capatosto, K., Wright, R. A., & Contractor, D. (2015). *State of the science: Implicit bias review 2015* (Vol. 3). Columbus, OH: Kirwan Institute for the Study of Race and Ethnicity.

Stack, L (2015, February 15). *American Muslims under attack.* The New York Times. https://www.nytimes.com/interactive/2015/12/22/us/Crimes-Against-Muslim-Americans.html

Swim, J. K., & Hyers, L. L. (1999). Excuse me—What did you just say?!: Women's public and private responses to sexist remarks. *Journal of Experimental Social Psychology,* 35(1), 68–88.

Swim, J. K., & Miller, D. L. (1999). White guilt: Its antecedents and consequences for attitudes toward affirmative action. *Personality and Social Psychology Bulletin,* 25(4), 500–514. https://doi.org/10.1177/0146167299025004008

Swim, J. K., & Stangor, C. (Eds.). (1998). *Prejudice: The target's perspective.* Elsevier.

Taylor, E. W. (1998). *The theory and practice of transformative learning: A critical review* (p. 8). Columbus: ERIC Clearinghouse on Adult, Career, and Vocational Education, Center on Education and Training for Employment, College of Education, the Ohio State University. http://hdl.voced.edu.au/10707/110722

Tupes, E. C., & Christal, R. E. (1992). Recurrent personality factors based on trait ratings. *Journal of Personality,* 60(2), 225–251. https://doi.org/10.1111/j.1467-6494.1992.tb00973.x

Tversky, A., & Kahneman, D. (1974). Judgment under uncertainty: Heuristics and biases. *Science,* 185, 1124–1131.

Vaid, J. (2009). Fair enough? Color and the commodification of self in Indian matrimonials. In E. N. Glenn (Ed.), *Shades of difference: Why skin color matters* (pp. 148–165). Stanford University Press.

Van den Berghe, P. L. (1978). Race and ethnicity: A sociobiological perspective. *Ethnic and Racial Studies,* 1(4), 401–411. https://doi.org/10.1080/01419870.1978.9993241

Van Dyne, L., & LePine, J. A. (1998). Helping and voice extra-role behaviors: Evidence of construct and predictive validity. *Academy of Management Journal,* 41(1), 108–119. https://doi.org/10.5465/256902

van Gorder, A. C. (2007). Pedagogy for the children of the oppressors: Liberative education for social justice among the world's privileged. *Journal of Transformative Education,* 5(1), 8–32. https://doi.org/10.1177/1541344607299854

Waldron, V. R. (1999). Communication practices of leaders, members, and protégés: The case of upward influence tactics. In M. E. Roloff (Eds.), *Communication yearbook 22* (pp. 251–299). Thousand Oaks, CA: Sage. https://doi.org/10.4324/9780203856826

Waldron, V. R., Hunt, M. D., & Dsilva, M. (1993). Towards a threat management model of upward communication: A study of influence and maintenance tactics in the leader-member dyad. *Communication Studies*, 44, 254–270. https://doi.org/10.1080/10510979309368399

Wang, Z., Walther, J. B., Pingree, S., & Hawkins, R. P. (2008). Health information, credibility, homophily, and influence via the Internet: Web sites versus discussion groups. *Health Communication*, 23(4), 358–368. https://doi.org/10.1080/10410230802229738

Wanous, J. P., Reichers, A. E., & Hudy, M. J. (1997). Overall job satisfaction: How good are single-item measures? *Journal of Applied Psychology*, 82(2), 247. https://doi.org/10.1037/0021-9010.82.2.247

Watkins, E. R. (2015). Mindfulness in the context of processing model theory. In K. W. Brown, J. D. Creswell, & R. M. Ryan (Eds.), *Handbook of mindfulness: Theory, research, and practice* (pp. 90–111). Guilford.

Wegener, D. T., & Petty, R. E. (1997). The flexible correction model: The role of naive theories of bias in bias correction. *Advances in Experimental Social Psychology*, 29, 141–208.

West, C., & Fenstermaker, S. (1995). Doing difference. *Gender and Society*, 9, 8–37. https://doi.org/10.1177/089124395009001002

Wilson, S. R. (1995). Elaborating the cognitive rules model of interaction goals: The problem of accounting for individual differences in goal formation. In B. Burleson (Ed.), *Communication yearbook 18* (pp. 3–25). Erlbaum.

Wilson, S. R. (2002). *Seeking and resisting compliance: Why people say what they do when trying to influence others*. Sage. https://doi.org/10.4135/9781452233185

Wilson, S. R., & Kunkel, A. W. (2000). Identity implications of influence goals: Similarities in perceived face threats and facework across sex and close relationships. *Journal of Language and Social Psychology*, 19, 195–221. https://doi.org/10.1177/0261927x00019002002

Yeung, E. (2015). *White and beautiful: An examination of skin whitening practices and female empowerment in China*. Columbia Academic Commons. https://academiccommons.columbia.edu/doi/10.7916/D8125S64

Zweig, C., & Wolf, S. (2009). *Romancing the shadow: A guide to soul work for a vital, authentic life*. Wellspring/Ballantine.

Author Index

Abrams, J. A., 100
Adair, J. K., 45
Albrecht, T. L., 32
Anderson, S. K., 45
Andrews, K., 100
Arndt, J., 105
Arudou, D., 100
Ashburn-Nardo, L., 7, 43
Averill, J. R., 104

Babrow, A. S., 21, 80, 81, 90
Bales, R. F., 15, 16
Banaji, M. R., 16, 18–20, 51, 56, 57, 67, 68
Banning, J. H., 45
Barbee, A. P., 33
Bargh, J. A., 51
Barrett, L. F., 5
Baxter, L. A., 94
Beck, A. T., 23
Belgrave, F. Z., 100
Berger, C. R., 7, 14, 59
Berkowitz, L., 36
Bollier, T., 104
Bosson, J. K., 7, 31, 44, 103, 104
Botero, I. C., 58
Bowers, J. W., 70
Boyd, R. D., 44
Boyd, W. L., 45
Braun, V., 121

Brinthaupt, T., 76
Brown, P., 58, 68
Burgoon, J. K., 7, 16, 49, 50, 59, 74
Burleson, B. R., 32, 33, 98, 114, 115
Buzzanell, P. M., 58

Cacioppo, J. T., 5, 50, 51, 59
Cai, D. A., 62
Campbell, J., 34
Canary, D. J., 36
Castelli, L., 31
Chaiken, S., 50
Chartrand, T. L., 51
Chen, S., 50
Christal, R. E., 41, 43
Christopher, S., 45
Clark, D. A., 23
Clarke, V., 121
Conrad, K., 100
Conte, H. R., 36
Cooren, F., 56
Cramer, P., 35, 36, 39, 109, 110
Cranton, P., 44, 45
Creasy, M., 36, 37, 108
Crews, T. B., 42
Cuddy, A. J., 7, 16
Cunningham, M. R., 33
Curry-Stevens, A., 45
Czopp, A. M., 7, 43

Dardenne, B., 104
Dasgupta, N., 31
Dass-Brailsford, P., 45
de Boer, A. G., 70
DiAngelo, R., 99
Dillard, J. P., 5, 7, 13–15, 62, 67, 122
Dixon, A. R., 101
Dixon, T. L., 100
Doucet, F., 45
Dovidio, J. F., 31, 67
Dumont, M., 104

Eagly, A. H., 61
Eifler, K., 45
Esposito, L., 102

Fairhurst, G., 57
Fairhurst, G. T., 57
Falbe, C. M., 58
Fazio, R. H., 31, 68, 102
Feng, B., 30
Fenstermaker, S., 57
Fiske, S. T., 7, 16, 102, 103
Fleiss, J. L., 63
Flores, R., 100
Folger, J. P., 62

Gaertner, S. L., 67
Galinsky, A. D., 21
Gardner, D. G., 70
Geyer, C., 36, 37
Gigerenzer, G., 50
Gillette, D., 34
Girod, S., 56
Glick, P., 103
Goldberg, L. R., 41, 42
Goldsmith, D. J., 30, 98, 99, 114–16
Good, J. J., 31, 104
Gottman, J. M., 36
Grabov, V., 44
Greene, J. O., 19
Greenwald, A. G., 16, 18–20, 31, 51, 56, 57, 67, 68
Grenny, J., 114

Hale, C. A., 63
Hall, E. D., 114
Hample, D., 11, 12
Harden, J. M., 14, 62
Hare, P. A., 16
Harkins, S. G., 61
Herring, C., 100
Hertel, B. R., 100
Hewes, D. E., 62
Hilden, L. E., 102
Hill, C., 56, 57
Hochschild, J. L., 100
Hoffman, M. L., 105
Hogg, M. A., 19, 68
Hollis, J., 31, 34, 35, 108–10
Hudson, R., 41
Hughes, M., 100
Hull, R. F. C., 34
Hunter, M., 101
Hunter, M. L., 101
Hyers, L. L., 7

Insko, C. A., 68
Isaac, C., 55–57

Jablonski, N. G., 100, 101
Johnson, B. T., 61
Johnson, R. A., 34–36
Johnson, S. K., 55
Jost, J. T., 104
Jung, C. G., 33–35, 43

Kahneman, D., 5
Kang, J., 31
Kay, A. C., 104
Keith, V. M., 100
Kerssen-Griep, J., 45
Klaczynski, P. A., 50
Knight, A., 100
Koenig, A. M., 55, 57
Krieger, L. H., 31
Kunkel, A. W., 62

Langer, E. J., 7, 16, 49, 50, 59, 74
Lawrence, T., 33

Lazarus, B. N., 106
Lazarus, R. S., 106
Leonardo, Z., 99
LePine, J. A., 37
Levinson, S. C., 58, 68
Lewis, K. M., 100, 101
Lim, T. S., 70
Luchey, S., 108
Lupton, D., 80

MacGeorge, E. L., 30, 99, 114–16
Maxwell, M. L., 100
McCaulley, M. H., 41–43
McIntosh, P., 98, 99
McMillan, R., 114
Merriam, S., 45
Mezirow, J., 8, 44, 45
Middleton, V. A., 45
Miller, D. L., 102
Mo, C. H., 57
Monk, Jr, E. P., 100
Moore, R., 34
Mortenson, S., 31, 33, 36, 37, 46, 55, 76, 102, 108, 110, 115
Mortenson, S. T., 33
Moskowitz, G. B., 7, 50
Mumby, D. K., 56, 57
Myers, I. B., 41–43
Myers, J. G., 44

Nagy, M. S., 70
Norwood, C., 100

O'Keefe, B. J., 14
Oliver, M. B., 102
Ostrom, E., 24, 25

Patterson, K., 114–16
Pearce, K. A., 94
Pearce, W. B., 94
Petty, R. E., 5, 50, 51, 59, 61, 68
Pinel, E. C., 31, 44
Plutchik, R., 36
Poole, M. S., 62
Putnam, L. L., 56

Ragins, B. R., 7, 16
Ramasubramanian, S., 102
Reeves, P., 45
Reskin, B., 31
Richo, D., 31, 104, 105, 108, 109
Riso, D. R., 41
Roets, A., 91
Romano, V., 102
Rudman, L. A., 31, 104
Rutland, A., 31

Samp, J. A., 67
Sandberg, S., 6
Saraswati, L. A., 100
Schopler, J., 68
Segrin, C., 14, 62
Seltzer, R., 100
Senge, P. M., 116
Shi, X., 1, 2, 5, 7, 14–17, 24, 55, 58, 74
Sillars, A. L., 36
Skagerlund, K., 59
Smith, R. C., 100
Solomon, D. H., 67
Sommers-Flanagan, J., 90
Sommers-Flanagan, R., 90
Staats, C., 31
Stack, L., 105
Stangor, C., 102
Stohl, C., 56, 57
Swim, J. K., 7, 102
Switzler, A., 114

Taylor, E. W., 8, 44, 45
Taylor, S. E., 7, 16
Telles, E., 100
Telles, E. E., 101
Terry, D. J., 19, 68
Tomelleri, S., 31
Tupes, E. C., 41, 43
Tversky, A., 5

Vaid, J., 100
Van den Berghe, P. L., 102
Van Dyne, L., 37, 58

van Gorder, A. C., 45
Vandello, J. A., 31, 44

Waldron, V. R., 55, 58, 59
Wang, Z., 116
Wanous, J. P., 70
Weaver, T., 42
Weaver, V., 100
Wegener, D. T., 7
West, C., 57
Williams, K. D., 61

Wilson, S. R., 7, 13, 17, 50, 55, 58, 62, 67
Winkel, D. E., 7, 16
Wolf, S., 35, 36

Yeung, E., 100
Yukl, G., 58

Zhang, Y., 100
Zogmaister, C., 31
Zweig, C., 35, 36

Subject Index

The Action Assembly Theory, 19
AIM. *See* Argumentative Interaction Management (AIM) framework
alternating process concept, 24
anxiety, 106
Anxious Controlling, 43
appreciation-oriented alternating communication process, 93
appreciation-oriented alternating inquiries, 13, 22–23; alternating communication process, 24; alternating motion and better-than-rational outcome, 24–25; emotional factor, 23–24
appreciative expressions, 88–89
appropriate anger, 104–5
appropriate fear, 106
appropriate guilt, 105
arguing, 11; argumentative interactions. *See* argumentative interaction process; user friendly strategy, 13
Argumentative Interaction Management (AIM) framework, 7, 12, 13; chain of interactions, 25–26; communication barriers, 13; core components and relationships, 26; implicit attitudes awareness, 18; interpersonal communication assumptions, 17–18; interpersonal influence, 13; . *See also individual entries*

argumentative interaction process, 7, 12, 83; co-creating social thoughts, 12; intrinsic interdependency between arguing parties, 12; persuasion focus, 12
arousal management goals, 14
automaticity in communication, 50–52
automatic reactions to situation, 52–53
automatic thinking mode, 20
"automatic white preference" mindset, 19

benevolent prejudice, corrosive kindness of, 101–4
benevolent racism, 102
benevolent sexism, 103–4
biased communication, 9, 20, 57, 67, 75
biased thinking, 18; cognitive schemas, 19–20; goal formation stage, 19; latent mindset, 18–19; recognize implicit biases, 20
The Big Five, 42
"blind spots" in thinking, 18

caution thoughts, 20
chaotic argumentative interaction, 18
closure, need for closure, 90–91
co-creating thoughts, 12
cognitive ease, 5; in communication, 5–7

cognitive elaboration, 49–50
cognitive reappraisal, 23–24
collaborative level, 7, 18, 26
color-blind approach, 118
colorism, 99
communication, 89; cognitive ease, 5–7; goals, 14–15; as intervention, 3–4, *4*; mindfulness in, 48, 59; rational choice models, 7; reactive communication, 21; relational communication, 87
communication with ease, 3
communicative interactions, 57
conflict formation, 84
conflict interaction management, *92*; appreciative expressions, 88–89; committing to closure, 90–93; creating external focal point, 89–90; overcoming the impulse to react immediately, 87–88
conflict management, 94
conflicts in relationships, 77–78
contrasting, 115
conventional wisdom, 25
coordinated action, 17
Coordinated Management of Meaning Theory, 94
correlational analysis, 37
COVID-19 pandemic, 47

debiasing, 20
deep personality assessment, 42
defusing shadow projections: calling out projection, 112–13; choosing emotion, 113; naming and claiming, 112; paying attention to intense feelings, 112
defusing shadow triggers, 107; choosing behavior, 108; discern emotions, 107; identifying shadow, 107; self-talk, 107
deliberative planning, 14; components, 14–15
disorienting dilemma, 31
dual-processing, 5
dynamism, 84

ease in communication, 3–4, 27; sensing features, 27
emotional charge, 31
emotional defenses, 1, 8
emotional efficacy, sense of, 33
emotional obstacles: knowing and doing, emotional disconnect, 32–33; preventing effective communication, 31–32; psychological shadow, 33–34; shadow activation, 35; shadow projection, 35–41
emotion-avoidant support goals, 33
emotion-based activities, 44
emotion-focused support goals, 33
evaluative orientations, 21, 22
explicit-reminder technique, 75
expressing disagreement scenarios, 11
external focal point, 89–90
"externalizing conversation" method, 90
externalizing therapy, 90

facet of automaticity, 51
"fast" thinking system, 5
feelings of guilt, 105
field effect, 16

gain perspective, 17, 77, 79, 94
gender-related implicit bias, 55
"give-and-take," ongoing negotiation of, 7, 18
goals, 13–14
Goals-Plans-Action (GPA) model, 13; communication goals, 13–15; strategic communication, theoretical perspective, 15

heuristic-automatic processing, 50
heuristics, 50; planning, 14
hidden preferences, 3, 16, 75–76
human attributes, 17–18

IAs. *See* implicit attitudes (IAs)
IAT. *See* Implicit Attitudes Test (IAT)
implicit attitudes (IAs), 18–19, 55, 56, 59; and communication, 56–57
Implicit Attitudes Test (IAT), 19, 56, 57

Subject Index

implicit biases, 20, 102
inappropriate anger, 104–5
inappropriate fear, 106
inappropriate guilt, 105–6
influence: interpersonal influence, 7, 13; upward influence, 55
inquiry-oriented alternating communication, 23
interpersonal arguing, 22
interpersonal influence, 7, 13; contemporary research, 16
interpersonal intervention, scenarios for, 29–31
intervention messages, *4*
intuitive thinking, 1
issue-relevant thinking, 3, 50, 74

mindful communication, 48, 49, 75; automaticity in communication, 50–52; cognitive elaboration, 49–50
mindfulness in communication, 48, 59
mindless behavior, 50
mutual influence system, 15
mutual modification, 22
Myers-Briggs, 42

negative self-talk, 24
"no-brainer" solution, 20

personality assessments, 43
perspective-taking (PT) process, 21, *92*; comfort in relationship, 86–87; situated *versus* evolving, context as, 83–86; uncovering probabilistic expectations, 81–83
persuasion goal, 15
plans, 14
politeness theory, 68
positive feelings, 5
potential threat, responses to, 23
pressure, 62
probabilistic orientations, 81
problematic integration (PI) theory, 21, 80; interpersonal communication, 22
problem-focused support goals, 33
process *versus* product analogy to conflict, *84*
projection, 35–37
psychological shadow, 33–34

racial discrimination, 101
rational choice models, 7, 16
reactive communication, 21
reappraisal, 22, 24
reason-based activities, 44
reasoning, 12, 13, 15, 25, 48, 62
reflexive thematic analysis, 121
relational communication, 87
relationships: comfort in, 86–87; conflicts in, 77–78

self-categorization theorists, 68
shadow activation, 35
shadow projection, 35, 104; characteristics, 39–40; conflict strategies, 36; correlational analysis, 37; defusing steps. *See* defusing shadow projections; negative attributions, 37; and negative teamwork behaviors, *40*; and positive teamwork behaviors, *38*; predator/victim projection identification, 110–11; projecting our own flaws onto others, 109–10; regression analyses, *41*; self-judgment, identifying projections of, 108–9; teammate projection, 39; trademark qualities, 36; unmet need projection identification, 111
shadows of confrontation, 113–14; setting goals, 114
shadow triggers, 104; appropriate and inappropriate anger, 104–5; appropriate and inappropriate fear, 106; appropriate and inappropriate guilt, 105–6; defusing steps. *See* defusing shadow triggers
short-term commitment, 91
skillful communicator, 17
"slow" thinking system, 5

Social Interaction Theory, 15; dimensions, 15; mutual influence system, 15; parsimonious theoretical framework, 16
strategic actors, 16
strategy-as-practice, 56
Strengths and Shadows Deep Assessment, 41; assessing unconscious side of personality, 42–44; strategic and interpersonal approach to personality, 42; vital and disorienting dilemma, 44–45
Strengths Quest and True Colors tests, 42
supportive confrontation, 30, 31, 46, 99
supportive confrontation messages, 114–15; defusing defensive emotions, 115; inviting target into collaboration, 116–18; speaking toward mutual purpose, 115–16
supportive confrontation reports, 120–21; choosing confrontation objectives, 122–23; describing and managing personal shadows, 123–24; engaging in confrontation, 124–25; outcomes, 125–27; sizing up situation, 121–22

supportive confrontation strategies: being supportive and speaking toward mutuality, 119–20; choosing objective for confrontation, 119; exploratory qualitative analysis. *See* supportive confrontation reports; identifying confrontation shadow, 119; knowing shadow around confrontation, 119
systematic thinking, 5

teammate projection, 39
Thinking, Fast and Slow (Kahneman), 5
thought-listing procedure, 14
transformative education, goal of, 45
transformative learning theory, 8, 44

upward influence, 55; biased communication, 74–75; hidden-preference tendencies, 75–76; internal and external noises, 75–76; mindful communication, 73–74; mindfulness, 59, 74; response to biases, 76; study I, 60–67; study II, 67–72

white fragility, 98
white privilege, 98–99

About the Authors

Xiaowei Shi received her PhD in communication from Purdue University in 2009. She is currently associate professor in the Department of Communication Studies at Middle Tennessee State University. Her research focuses on influence processes and supportive message production in contexts of professional and close relationships.

Her research findings have been cited over 200 times in peer publications and have earned her four "Top-Paper" awards from the National Communication Association's Annual Conventions.

Steve Mortenson is associate professor and an award-winning teacher and researcher. He has taught at the University of Delaware since 2003. His research and teaching focus on personality assessment and intervention, teamwork studies, emotional management, leadership development, and interpersonal effectiveness. He designs and conducts leadership and communication seminars for the Blue Hen Leadership Program, the National Association of Environmental Management, Gore, Amtrak, the Horn Institute, Christiana Hospital and the US State Department's international programs for young leaders in the Middle East (MEPI), and women from Sub-Saharan countries in Africa (SUSI). He lives in Newark, Delaware, with his wife and their two dogs.

www.ingramcontent.com/pod-product-compliance
Lightning Source LLC
Chambersburg PA
CBHW021357300426
44114CB00012B/1268